Flexibility-Based Cognitive Behaviour Therapy

In this book, Windy Dryden brings together the four major strands that have shaped his idiosyncratic approach to clinical practice – (i) Cognitive Behaviour Therapy; (ii) flexibility in practice; (iii) Rational Emotive Behaviour Therapy; and (iv) pluralism – an approach he calls 'Flexibility-Based Cognitive Behaviour Therapy'.

Perhaps uniquely for the literature, this volume provides an extended account of how a world-leading therapist personally thinks about and practises psychotherapy. As well as insights from over 40 years as a therapist, the book reflects the most recent developments in Dryden's work, and highlights both the different theories he is using and the core building blocks of his practice.

Aimed at therapists in training and practice, *Flexibility-Based Cognitive Behaviour Therapy* presents a rare opportunity to gain an insight from one of the leading figures in the field of psychotherapy.

Windy Dryden is in part-time clinical and consultative practice and is an international authority on Cognitive Behaviour Therapy. He is Emeritus Professor of Psychotherapeutic Studies at Goldsmiths, University of London. He has worked in psychotherapy for more than 40 years and is the author of over 220 books.

Flexibility-Based Cognitive Behaviour Therapy

Insights from 40 Years of Practice

Windy Dryden

LONDON AND NEW YORK

First published 2018
by Routledge
2 Park Square, Milton Park, Abingdon, Oxon OX14 4RN

and by Routledge
711 Third Avenue, New York, NY 10017

Routledge is an imprint of the Taylor & Francis Group, an informa business

© 2018 Windy Dryden

The right of Windy Dryden to be identified as author of this work
has been asserted by him in accordance with sections 77 and 78 of
the Copyright, Designs and Patents Act 1988.

All rights reserved. No part of this book may be reprinted or
reproduced or utilised in any form or by any electronic, mechanical,
or other means, now known or hereafter invented, including
photocopying and recording, or in any information storage or
retrieval system, without permission in writing from the publishers.

Trademark notice: Product or corporate names may be trademarks
or registered trademarks, and are used only for identification and
explanation without intent to infringe.

British Library Cataloguing in Publication Data
A catalogue record for this book is available from the British Library

Library of Congress Cataloguing in Publication Data
A catalog record for this book has been requested

ISBN: 978-0-8153-7159-5 (hbk)
ISBN: 978-0-8153-7157-1 (pbk)
ISBN: 978-1-351-24642-2 (ebk)

Typeset in Times New Roman
by Swales & Willis Ltd, Exeter, Devon, UK

Contents

	Preface	vi
1	Rigidity and flexibility	1
2	Effective bonds in therapy	9
3	Shared views in therapy	18
4	Negotiated and agreed goals in therapy	32
5	Goal-directed tasks in therapy	46
6	The importance of context in FCBT	61
7	Working with rigid and flexible attitudes and mindsets in therapy	78
8	Working with extreme and non-extreme attitudes in therapy	90
9	The change process in therapy	110
Appendix	The models of psychological disturbance and health that I use in my work	131
	Notes	135
	References	137
	Index	141

Preface

This book incorporates four major strands that have shaped my own idiosyncratic approach to clinical practice. As such, this volume represents an accurate picture of how I personally think about and practise psychotherapy. I refer to the approach that I take as 'Flexibility-Based Cognitive Behaviour Therapy'. I do so (1) because my approach is broadly CBT in orientation and (2) because the concept of flexibility is at the heart of both my thinking and practice of therapy. Indeed, in my view, it is at the core of psychological health. As such, my own goals as a psychotherapist are to promote flexibility in my clients, both in terms of their attitudes and their behaviour. 'Flexibility', therefore, is the first major feature of my clinical practice.

I am perhaps best known for being a 'Rational Emotive Behaviour Therapist' and if I were to nail my colours to any therapeutic mast it would be to REBT. Indeed, I am happy to teach REBT to other professionals as long as I am clear that I am doing just that and not necessarily representing the fullness of my clinical practice. On the other hand, there is something limiting when one conceives of oneself as a practitioner of any specific approach to therapy and also when one represents oneself publicly in this way. Thus, while the theory and practice of REBT is the second major strand that has shaped my idiosyncratic approach to clinical practice, it does not completely define my work as a psychotherapist, as I will make clear later.

The third major strand underpinning my practice is the 'working alliance' theory originated by Ed Bordin (1979). This is a framework that helps clinicians to think broadly about their work with clients with respect to therapeutic bonds, views, goals and tasks. Briefly:

- *bonds* refer to the interpersonal connectedness between the therapist and client;
- *views* refer to the understandings that both participants have on salient issues;
- *goals* refer to the purpose of the therapeutic meetings;
- *tasks* refer to the procedures carried out by both therapist and client in the service of the latter's goals.

I have devoted a chapter to each of these components because of their importance in shaping my thinking and intervening in the consulting room.

The final strand that has shaped my clinical thinking and practice is that of pluralism (Cooper & McLeod, 2011). Here, in particular, I have been influenced by the idea that fully involving the client in the clinical decision-making process is both practically sound, ethically desirable and liberating for the client, once he or she has become accustomed to the idea! This is not to say that I downplay my professional expertise. Rather, it means that such expertise as I have is connected to what the client brings to the therapeutic setting in terms of their expertise, strengths, resources, etc. As I see it, psychotherapy, then, is a fusion between what I bring to the endeavour and what the client brings to the endeavour. The important point is that both contributions are acknowledged and that there is a mechanism for resolving differences between therapist and client as therapy unfolds.

It is perhaps useful to the reader if I make clear what I am *not* going to do in this book. First, I am not going to present protocols for the treatment of a variety of clinical disorders. Second, I am not going to describe clinical techniques. Indeed, I would say that this book is light on technique and heavy on framework and ideas. Instead, my goal is to provide a feel for the way I work and for the strands that have shaped this work.

As I mentioned above, I refer to my approach as 'Flexibility-Based Cognitive Behaviour Therapy'. However, the last thing that I want to do is to add yet another therapeutic approach to a crowded field. However, my approach is flexible, I believe, and it is most closely related to the psychotherapeutic tradition known as Cognitive Behaviour Therapy (CBT), hence the book's title.

Chapter 1

Rigidity and flexibility

Flexibility-Based Cognitive Behaviour Therapy (FCBT) is based on the concept of flexibility. To understand flexibility I would like you to consider its antonym, which is rigidity. By adopting a rigid approach to phenomena we end up with a fixed view about how such phenomena absolutely should or must be. We may take action to try to force these phenomena to fit into the fixed categories we have established in our minds, if they are not in any way as we insist in our mind that they must be.

1.1 Procrustes

Let me start by giving you an example from Greek mythology. A certain Procrustes had a house by the side of the road and offered hospitality and a bed for the night to passing strangers. He would invite them to dine with him and then to sleep the night. Procrustes was rigid in his insistence that everybody should fit into his one size fits all bed. Because he had this rigid view, he would stretch the legs of those guests who were too short for the bed and cut off the legs of those who proved too tall for it. All this was because Procrustes was rigid about having his guests fit into his bed. In fact, the phrase 'fitting something into a Procrustean bed' is derived from this story. But justice finally reigned: Procrustes had a dose of his own medicine when Theseus adjusted him to his own bed.

Now, let's imagine what would have happened had Procrustes been flexible in his approach towards having guests sleep in his bed. First, he would have let them sleep in his bed without trying to 'adjust' them in any way. If he had only wanted people who fitted his bed exactly, he would only have invited people he knew would fit the bed. Moreover, he might have ordered different-sized beds to allow his guests to be comfortable. Had Procrustes done all this, Theseus would have had no reason to exact justice by killing him.

2 Rigidity and flexibility

The story of Procrustes – and my proposed alternative – clearly demonstrates the consequences of rigidity and flexibility. The rigid stance of Procrustes led to the death of his guests and eventually to his own death. He was unable to think of a creative way to solve his 'bed-size' problem and his rigidity led to 'black and white thinking': 'Either you fit my bed or I will make you fit my bed one way or another.' Had Procrustes adopted a flexible approach, however, he would have engaged in creative, lateral thinking, his guests would have lived and he would have lived. By being flexible he would have adopted a form of 'grey' thinking rather than 'black and white' thinking, as represented by the thought: 'There are a variety of solutions to the problem if you don't fit my bed.'

1.2 Rigidity and flexibility in psychological functioning

Procrustes' story still has much to teach us both about psychological disturbance and how to address it. I will deal with each of these issues one at a time. First, I will examine the impact of rigidity and flexibility on psychological functioning.

Albert Ellis (1913–2007) was the founder of Rational Emotive Behaviour Therapy (REBT) and I have practised this approach, in my own way, for over 40 years. Ellis argued that psychological disturbance is based on 'absolutistic' thinking[1] (Ellis & Joffe Ellis, 2011) and that psychological health is based on 'nondemanding' thinking[2] (Ellis & Joffe Ellis, 2011). I have been deeply influenced by his views on this subject.

1.2.1 The impact of rigidity on psychological functioning

I will show what the impact of rigidity is on psychological functioning by providing an example. Sarah's approach to achievement at work is rigid. If her work performance is good, she will be pleased as long as it continues to be good. However, although her performance is good, she becomes anxious if she thinks anything might prevent her achievements at work from continuing. Sarah's problem started when her work performance deteriorated. At this point, she became disturbed psychologically because her attitude to achievement is rigid and therefore for Sarah the failure to achieve is not an option. However, the problem is that it is an option in reality. Therefore, as this reality began to occur, Sarah had no capacity in her mind to deal with it in a constructive way because of her mental rigidity. This rigidity led her to form one or more extreme conclusions, for instance:

Rigidity and flexibility   3

- 'When I don't achieve at work it's the end of the world' (which is known as an awfulising attitude).
- 'Not achieving at work is something I can't put up with' (which is known as a discomfort intolerance attitude).
- 'When I don't achieve at work I'm a failure' (which is known as a self-devaluation attitude).

When it came to her behaviour, Sarah's rigid response to her non-achievement at work led to a dual response. Sometimes she gave up, while at other times she would redouble her efforts, thus risking her health through overwork. Which of these two paths she took depended, partly, on how her rigidity impacted on the type of extreme attitude she held and the inferential thinking it subsequently resulted in. Inferential thinking is characterised by interpretation and prediction, in this case coloured by rigidity. When Sarah's rigidity caused her to think that non-achievement proved she was a failure (extreme, self-devaluation attitude) and that she would never succeed at work (subsequent inferential thinking), she was prone to give up. On the other hand, when Sarah's rigidity caused her to think that her failure to achieve was not an option and that it should be avoided at all costs (extreme awfulising attitude) and that she would not allow anything to impede the achievement of her goals (subsequent inferential thinking), she would tend to overwork, putting her health in jeopardy. Sarah alternated between these two responses, depending upon how things were going at work and which extreme attitude and subsequent inferential thinking she was engaged in at the time.

1.2.2 The impact of flexibility on psychological functioning

I have emphasised that flexibility is the healthy alternative to rigidity. Let us examine how the adoption of a flexible approach to work achievement would make a difference to Sarah. If Sarah adopted a flexible perspective to work achievement, then if she performs well at work, she will be satisfied as long as she continues to perform well. She may become concerned (rather than anxious) if she thinks anything might threaten her work achievements from continuing. This concern will help her engage in productive problem-solving to prevent any threats that may be looming and to handle constructively any threats that may materialise. If Sarah's work achievement ceased then her flexible mind would enable her to deal with this possibility healthily because, while it might be undesirable, she has not excluded the possibility of a lack of achievement at work from her mind. As such, Sarah would have the mental facility to

4 Rigidity and flexibility

handle it constructively. Her flexibility would enable her to make one or more of the following non-extreme conclusions:

- 'If I don't achieve at work, it's bad but it isn't the end of the world' (this is known as a non-awfulising attitude).
- 'Although it is a struggle to cope with non-achievement at work, I can put up with it and it is worth my while for me to do so' (this is known as a discomfort tolerance attitude).
- 'If I don't achieve at work I am not a failure. Instead, I am a complex, unrateable fallible human being who at the moment is not succeeding' (this is known as an unconditional self-acceptance attitude).

Regarding her behaviour, in response to not achieving at work Sarah's flexible standpoint will lead her to act in a number of ways. Compare this with the split in her response when she takes a rigid standpoint. If she is flexible she will first look for the source of her difficulty and then take remedial action based on a reasonable assessment of her problem. She may, for example, decide she needs to learn a new skill and in this case will enrol on an appropriate training course. Alternatively, she may decide that she has a personal difficulty that is preventing her from progressing. In that case she will take the appropriate steps to address this difficulty, by seeking counselling or coaching, for example, depending on the nature of the difficulty. She may also seek help from her workplace or decide that she should take steps of her own to get back on track. In other words, she has a variety of options, all of them designed to encourage her to handle the obstacle and allow her to improve her work performance. This approach contrasts with a black and white attitude in dealing with the problem stemming from a rigid mental attitude. In this later case, as you may recall, she will either tend to give up or to work in an unhealthy way to get back on track.

Sarah's constructive responses are based on her non-extreme attitudes and her subsequent realistic inferential thinking. Both of these will arise from a flexible approach.

1.3 Rigidity and flexibility in the practice of psychotherapy

If you survey the whole field of psychotherapy, it will soon become clear to you that there are many different approaches. Specific approaches exist within the traditions such as psychodynamic, humanistic, cognitive-behavioural, transpersonal and systemic, as well as therapies that aim to combine or integrate these approaches. This way of working is known as eclecticism, psychotherapy integration or pluralistic practice.

Concepts of rigidity and flexibility are relevant to the above areas. It is possible, for instance, to practise a specific approach to therapy either in a flexible or rigid way and my hypothesis is that experienced practitioners within these approaches are more flexible in their use of them than novice therapists who are more likely to practise their particular approach in a more rigid, by-the-book form.

Those practitioners who consider themselves advocates of eclecticism, psychotherapy integration or pluralism tend to view themselves as practising therapy in a flexible manner and this is probably the case to the extent that they show no commitment to any specific approach to therapy. However, if we take a closer look at the practice of the latter, it will soon become obvious that they do favour particular approaches over others. However, depending on the extent that they exclude specific approaches, one might well ask why they are excluding or downplaying these approaches. For instance, many training programmes devoted to integrative approaches to counselling and psychotherapy, either tend to exclude or downplay cognitive-behavioural elements. This seems strange considering that among the different specific approaches within psychotherapy, CBT has perhaps the best evidence base. Could this be a sign of rigidity? It is perhaps difficult to say, but to underplay or exclude an approach that has a good evidence base may suggest this.

1.3.1 What does it mean to practise an approach rigidly and flexibly?

Every psychotherapeutic approach has practical procedural rules. In REBT, therefore, a treatment sequence outlines a particular order in which interventions should be made (Dryden, DiGiuseppe & Neenan, 2010). In person-centred therapy, therapists are encouraged to work within clients' frame of reference. Its practitioners are consequently discouraged from asking questions as these may come from the therapist's frame of reference rather than that of the client's.

When these rules are applied rigidly, an REBT practitioner would only adopt the recommended sequence even where there was evidence that this sequence was not working. In person-centred therapy, a therapist who never asks questions is considered to be rigid, particularly in cases where asking a question may progress the therapy. Thus, rigidity in

6 Rigidity and flexibility

psychotherapy occurs when practitioners adhere dogmatically to rules of procedure and exclude specific interventions that could be helpful even if not generally recommended by the particular approach.

What, in contrast, are the markers of flexibility? Let me be clear: I do not equate flexibility in the practice of psychotherapy with being laissez-faire in the sense that anything goes. Neither do I mean that all approaches are given equal weight when considering eclecticism or integration. Those practitioners who favour specific ways of working, particularly when there is evidence in favour of these ways, are acting ethically by explaining this point to their clients. They are, however, being flexible by including methods in their practice they do not necessarily favour when it is indicated that they should do so. Therefore, practitioners are being flexible when they have preferred ways of working but are prepared to make compromises with their preferences.

1.4 The concepts of flexibility and rigidity in Flexibility-Based CBT

In this book, I use the phrase 'Flexibility-Based CBT' (FCBT) to describe the way I work for two reasons.

1 It asserts that flexibility is the basis of healthy functioning and that my goal is to promote flexibility in my clients – flexibility in cognitive functioning, in behavioural responding and in pursuing their goals and acting on their values.

2 I have used the term FCBT because it advocates flexibility in therapeutic response. As I see promoting flexibility in psychological functioning as a major goal, I therefore favour therapeutic techniques that advance this goal, but because FCBT is flexible as a major therapeutic principle, it enables me to make compromises with my favoured strategies and techniques when it is in my client's interests to do so.

1.4.1 Is it possible to practise FCBT rigidly?

'Yes' is the short answer to this question. The founder of Rational Emotive Behaviour Therapy (REBT) Albert Ellis, whose ideas have greatly influenced my development as a psychotherapist, once said that any good idea can be turned bad by rigidity. So how may I avoid being rigid in the way I practise Flexibility-Based CBT (FCBT)? I think I can do so in the following ways.

1.4.1.1 Guarding against imposing flexibility as a goal on a client who is not interested in it

A rigid approach to things is comforting for some clients, who don't want to become more flexible. I would acknowledge, as a therapist, that in my opinion, the client would be better served by learning to become more flexible and I might make this case to the client. On the other hand, I would accept the client's explanation and help them in the way they want to be helped provided this did not endanger the client's life or well-being. I would not impose flexibility on disinterested clients.

1.4.1.2 Using non-preferred strategies and techniques and making compromises with my preferences

I begin by using techniques that best facilitate flexibility and I carry on with these techniques to give the client every chance to use them and to get the most out of them. However, when it becomes clear that the client is not benefiting from these preferred techniques I will stop using these methods. Rather than being driven by my allegiance to the ideal practice of what I call FCBT, I would be driven by my allegiance to the client. According to an apocryphal story, a trainee psychoanalyst once said: 'The beauty of psychoanalysis is that even though the patient is not improving at least you have the comfort of knowing that you are doing the right thing.' This viewpoint is anathema to me: as a flexible therapist, I object both to the smugness of this statement and to its rigidity.

1.5 Pluralism and Flexibility-Based CBT

As there are echoes of the concept of pluralism in what I have written in this chapter up until now, let me make clear the pluralistic roots of my practice.

1   What I call Flexibility-Based CBT belongs within the cognitive-behavioural tradition of psychotherapy. However, I am respectful of other approaches both within and outside this tradition. Respect of this kind is an important feature of pluralism (Cooper & McLeod, 2011).
2   While I agree with the Stoic view of Epictetus that: 'People are disturbed not by things, but by the views that they take of things' and while I privilege the role of rigidity in accounting for disturbance, I also agree fundamentally with the pluralistic view that there are many pathways to psychological change. I am guided by both these ideas in clinical practice.

8 Rigidity and flexibility

3   I concur with Cooper and McLeod's (2011) pluralistic views that taking seriously clients' views regarding what is helpful to them in therapy, even if these views are not compatible with the way I think clinically and how I practise, is paramount to the practice of therapy. Although I may not go as far as Cooper and McLeod (2011) in privileging the views of clients, I agree with them that engaging clients in an explicit meta-therapeutic dialogue with clients is important and I endeavour to do this in my work.

4   Burns (1980) has listed a number of cognitive distortions considered present in depression and other emotional disorders. One such distortion is termed 'either/or' thinking. Ellis and Dryden (1997) hypothesised that this form of thinking (and the other cognitive distortions) tend to arise from sticking to rigid attitudes, and research tends to support this view (see Bond & Dryden, 1996a, 1996b). In contrast to cognitive distortions, balanced cognitions are considered to arise from sticking to flexible attitudes, and again there is research to support this hypothesis (see Bond & Dryden, 1996a, 1996b). 'Both/and' thinking is the balanced alternative to either/or thinking. Cooper and McLeod (2011) maintain that a defining aspect of a pluralistic approach to counselling and psychotherapy is its emphasis on a 'both/and' as opposed to an 'either/or' approach to therapeutic phenomena. Pluralism is certainly an important factor in both my clinical thinking and practice.

5   Cooper and McLeod (2011) also point out that reflexivity is one of the features of a pluralistic approach to counselling and psychotherapy. Reflexivity describes the practitioners' ability to reflect on the approach being used and by doing so to acknowledge both its strengths and its weaknesses. Flexibility, as we shall see, is connected to the concept of human fallibility. This latter concept acknowledges that approaches to counselling and psychotherapy have been developed by fallible human beings and may therefore be right and wrong in many ways. Such a pluralistic attitude views the development of counselling approaches as being rather like the development of self-actualisation – a journey towards greater truth which, in all probability, may never be fully realised.

Now that I have discussed the central concepts of flexibility and rigidity in FCBT, in the next four chapters I will discuss the important role that the working alliance plays in Flexibility-Based CBT, starting with therapeutic bonds.

Chapter 2

Effective bonds in therapy

I briefly described in the preface, the four components of the working alliance (Bordin, 1979) as follows:

- *bonds* refer to the interpersonal connectedness between therapist and client;
- *views* refer to the understandings that both participants have on salient issues;[1]
- *goals* refer to the purpose of therapeutic meetings;
- *tasks* refer to the procedures carried out by both therapist and client in the service of the latter's goals.

Although I will be dealing with each of these components separately in this book, please note that they are interconnected. In this chapter, I will discuss the importance of the bond between my client and myself in FCBT. In discussing these bonds, I will consider the following:

- the 'core conditions';
- the reflection process;
- interpersonal style;
- the bonds of influence; and
- transference and counter-transference.

2.1 The 'core conditions'

One of the most seminal articles in the psychotherapeutic literature, in my opinion, is Bordin's (1979) paper on the working alliance. But if that is the case, then possibly a paper published by Carl Rogers over 20 years earlier is perhaps *the* most seminal. In that 1957 article, Rogers argued that six conditions were necessary and sufficient for therapeutic personality change to occur. Over the subsequent years, three of these conditions have been regarded as core and are now therefore called the 'core conditions'.

In Rogers' original paper, these were known as empathy, unconditional positive regard[2] and genuineness. It is important to point out here that the presence of these conditions needs to be experienced by the client to enable them to have therapeutic potency.[3]

In general, I agree with my CBT colleagues that it is important for clients to experience their therapists as empathic, accepting[4] and genuine in their interactions with them, although particular 'core conditions' for some may be more therapeutic than for others. Thus, Susan, whom we will meet later in this book, valued my honesty more than she did my acceptance of her. This brings up the question of how I can tell which condition is valued more than others, and that leads us to a discussion of what I call the 'reflection process', which is a key aspect of the way I work.

2.2 The reflection process

I tend to follow what has become known as George Kelly's first principle, which states: 'If you want to know what is wrong with someone, ask them, they may tell you.' The version underlying the 'reflection process' is as follows: 'If you want to know what is right and wrong for a person, ask them, they may tell you.' As the reflection process is interactive, it not only incorporates my view, but that of my client. What is particularly therapeutic is what emerges from the ensuing discussion, particularly if I favour the client's viewpoint rather than my own.[5]

An example of the reflection process can be found in one of the Marx Brothers' movies, where Groucho stops the action to give a reflective commentary on what has just happened. In FCBT the reflection process is similar: my client and I reflect on what has happened, is happening, or may still happen between us. This process may be followed through formally, for example, in review sessions or end of session feedback or, more informally, during the therapy process.

I see this reflection process as a forum for my client and me to discuss matters pertaining to the therapy in which the client is involved. I used to consider this process to be 'extra to' or 'outside the therapy'. However, I now regard it as an integral aspect of the therapy. In that respect, it is a means of showing the state of the relationship with regard to the degree of acceptance, trust and mutual respect that is present in that relationship.

2.3 Interpersonal style

The interpersonal style adopted by my client and myself and the goodness of 'fit' between these respective styles is the third area that is relevant to how I work. According to working alliance theory the therapeutic

Effective bonds in therapy 11

bond can be enhanced when the 'fit' between my client and myself is good, while it can be threatened when this fit is poor.

Different approaches to therapy have posited preferred interpersonal styles between client and therapist. For instance, the preferred interpersonal style in Beck's Cognitive Therapy (CT) is for the two participants to collaborate actively in working with cognitive-behavioural elements of the client's problems. Beck contrasts this collaborative interpersonal style with a style that is more challenging, which he has associated previously with practitioners of Ellis's Rational Emotive Behaviour Therapy. This view is illustrated in the following contribution to the Academy of Cognitive Therapy Listserve:

> I notice that many of you have used the word 'challenge' in response to investigating patients' automatic thoughts, beliefs, and hallucinations. I wonder if this is really the appropriate word since it sounds confrontational. In practice, we all approach these phenomena with an investigative spirit (for instance guided discovery, collaborative empiricism). In other words, we do not imply that a patient's particular verbal production is wrong (as implied by the word 'challenge'), but we examine, evaluate, test, etc.
>
> (Academy of Cognitive Therapy listserve)

The client is viewed in pluralistic approaches to counselling and psychotherapy as being an active participant in the therapeutic process, but these approaches also recognise that either clients cannot or will not involve themselves actively in therapy, but instead prefer to adopt a more passive therapeutic style (Cooper & McLeod, 2011). I prefer an active, collaborative approach, but I will also modify my interpersonal style in order to provide a 'good enough fit' with that of my client. With some clients this may result in my adopting a challenging style, while with others more of a didactic, teaching style.

The interpersonal therapist styles, instead of existing as either/or categories, may vary along a continuum. I locate myself, according to client variability, on the common style dimensions:

- activity–inactivity;
- formality–informality;
- humour–seriousness;
- self-disclosure–non-self-disclosure.

Please note that I am not suggesting that, as an example, having decided to use self-disclosure with a client I would use it as the predominant

12   Effective bonds in therapy

therapeutic style, but rather that to make an appropriate point with that client when the opportunity presented itself, I would use self-disclosure when I might not do the same thing with another client.

2.3.1 Issues with respect to interpersonal style

To consider the issue of interpersonal style in therapy in full would require a complete volume of its own. However, for our present purposes, I will make the following points.

2.3.1.1 Gauging which interpersonal style to adopt

It is never easy to determine what would be the best interpersonal style to adopt with each client. However, following George Kelly's above suggestion, and as demonstrated in my work with Susan, I will ask the client directly:

Windy: Which interactive style would you prefer to ask your therapist to adopt so that he or she might get the most out of you as a client?

Susan: That's difficult to answer. I'm not quite sure what you mean . . .

Windy: Well, for instance, would you find it more helpful if I adopted a passive or an active interactive style?

Susan: I think an active one, provided you also allowed me to be active.

Windy: OK, that's fine. And would you prefer me to be more formal or informal?

Susan: Oh, informal, definitely. I'm not keen on formality.

Windy: And what about humour?

Susan: Well, I know therapy's a serious business, but I find humour can help, because it allows me to put things into perspective.

Windy: If I occasionally shared a little of my own experience, would that help if it shed light on how you might be able to address your own problems?

Susan: If it's relevant I would find that helpful. And it would also make me feel that I wasn't a freak.

From this exchange we have now ascertained that Susan considers she will find it most useful to her if I adopt an informal, active, self-disclosing, humorous style. Whether this actually proves to be the case has yet to be discovered, but it has established some provisional guidelines for

Effective bonds in therapy 13

proceeding with Susan in regard to my interactive style. This can be discussed by the therapist and client, as with other issues, as part of the reflection process that I have discussed earlier.

Such information may come to me from my clients in questionnaire form. For instance, with regard to the client's preferences relating to therapist interpersonal style, Lazarus (1989) in his Life History Questionnaire (LHQ) includes the following questions, which he routinely used to give his clients while he was in active practice:

- How do you think a therapist should interact with their clients?
- What personal qualities do you think the ideal therapist should possess?

I might add the following to these:

- If they are to get the most out of you as a client, which interactive style would you advise your therapist to adopt?
- When working with you, which interactive style would you advise your therapist not to adopt and why?

2.3.1.2 Adopting a style that does not reinforce clients' problems

In any interpersonal setting, when two people come together their interactive styles may complement each other's or may conflict in some way. However, just because such styles complement each other, it should not necessarily be assumed that effective therapy may therefore be enhanced. For such a 'mesh' may prove to be unproductive. Although I value an active-directive style, I appreciate that there may be a risk that such activity may 'pull' for client passivity. In cases where a client becomes passive this may in turn 'pull' me to become increasingly active. A vicious cycle may then be created if I am not careful and this may reflect and reinforce the client's everyday life passivity problems. I endeavour to be aware of the risks attached to adopting a therapeutic style that might reinforce my clients' problems and guard against this. As well as high levels of activity with a passive client, you should note the following examples of therapeutic styles that could particularly reinforce clients' problems or unhealthy modes of functioning. In such cases I also endeavour to avoid adopting these styles.

14 Effective bonds in therapy

2.3.1.2.1 GUARD AGAINST BEING UNDULY WARM WITH CLIENTS WHO HAVE A STRONG NEED FOR APPROVAL

Being unduly warm with clients may reinforce their need for my approval. I must therefore be less warm and to agree with the client that their need for approval is in itself a target for change.

2.3.1.2.2 GUARD AGAINST BEING UNDULY DIRECTIVE WITH CLIENTS WHO ARE HIGHLY REACTANT

Clients who are highly reactant have an adverse reaction to perceived or actual attempts to influence them. Because of this tendency, it is important for me to emphasise client choice more than I usually do. Should I fail to do so, my client may terminate therapy as a means to preserve their autonomy.

2.3.1.2.3 GUARD AGAINST USING HUMOUR WITH CLIENTS WHO USE HUMOUR AS A DEFENCE

As is well known, some people use humour as a means of protecting themselves against emotional pain and thus from dealing with their problems effectively. If I were to use humour with such a client, I would reinforce this tendency unwittingly. When humour is used effectively it helps promote therapeutic change, which will be apparent to both client and therapist. It is often introduced by clients themselves to help reinforce their defences and in such cases, I need to respond in a way that does not join in with the client's levity.

2.3.1.3 Therapist authenticity

In my work I have emphasised how important it is for the therapist to demonstrate interpersonal flexibility. This, however, should be done in a genuine way and although putting on an act for a client may not be noticed immediately, it will eventually be detected with negative effects on the working alliance. An effective therapist, according to Lazarus (1989), should be an 'authentic chameleon', which means in this context, that they are able to modify their interpersonal style from patient to patient, while doing so authentically. As part of my training I needed to become aware of my range of interpersonal styles and have the ability to employ this range at different stages of the therapy process in a genuine way with different clients.

2.4 The bonds of influence

Work emerging from social psychology in North America in the 1980s suggested that it would be useful to regard the therapeutic relationship as an interpersonal setting where influence may take place (Dorn, 1984). This approach did not prove to be popular with therapists, who are inclined to be uncomfortable with the idea that they influence their clients, and instead prefer to regard themselves as facilitators of their clients' growth. Although the 'counselling as influence' notion may be unpalatable to some, I regard it as a useful way of thinking about why clients take heed of their therapists, independent of the message the therapist may be trying to convey to them. As a key therapeutic task in my work is helping my clients adopt the view that flexibility in attitude is healthier for them than rigidity, 'counselling as influence' is particularly important to my practice.

While I am considering here how, as a therapist, I influence my clients, it would be more accurate to say that my clients allow me to influence them. And they do this for three main reasons:

1   They like me or find me *attractive* in some way.
2   They *trust* me.
3   They are impressed by my *credibility*, which may include my experience, expertise and/or credentials.

Let me illustrate what I mean here. What mattered to Susan, the client I am referring to in this book, was that as an author of two books on anxiety (Dryden, 2000, 2011a), I was thus regarded by her as an expert. Although she had consulted two other competent CBT therapists, Susan felt that they lacked the external signs of expertise that she valued.

Given this framework, I am inclined to ask clients the following question as part of the assessment process. Are you most likely to listen to a therapist and give credence to what they have to say (a) if you like the therapist as a person, (b) if you trust them or (c) if the person appears to know what they are talking about? I am then guided by their answer in deciding how best to influence them. I will strive to meet my clients' preferences regarding this as far as I can do so genuinely and as long as doing so is therapeutic for my clients.

Ideally, the content of what their therapists say should impress clients irrespective of whether clients like their therapists or whether therapists' expertise is demonstrable. However, how the messenger is perceived often determines the potency of the message in the real world of counselling and psychotherapy.

16 Effective bonds in therapy

As a therapist, trainer and supervisor my own experience is that some clients may heed those therapists they like and allow themselves to be influenced by them even if such therapists do not demonstrate expertise, while others may heed and allow themselves to be influenced by expert therapists, even if they may not like them. Few clients, however, will listen to therapists they do not trust even if they like them or are impressed by their credentials.

2.5 Transference and counter-transference

The final area relevant to the bond between my client and myself concerns the concepts of transference and counter-transference. Although these concepts derive from psychoanalytic approaches to psychotherapy (see Jacobs, 2017), the phenomena indicated by these terms are more significant than the use of the terms themselves. The terms indicate that both my client and myself bring to the therapeutic relationship tendencies to perceive, feel and act towards another person that are influenced by their previous interactions with significant others. Such tendencies often have a profound influence on how the working alliance is developed and maintained.

2.5.1 Transference

I will deal with the issue of transference following Miranda and Andersen's (2007) social-cognitive model. I first ask my client to name and describe significant others and to refer in particular to facets of their interpersonal relations, particularly problematic issues. Once I have identified these representations, I will be able to see when these are activated in the therapeutic relationship and help my client see the link between the representations of significant others and their present response to me as therapist. With the help of the client particular cues in my behaviour need to be identified. I will apologise as a clinician, for any unintended insensitivity as this does help promote the use of the reflection process, which is so necessary when clients process transferential experiences.

2.5.2 Counter-transference

Unhelpful therapist schemas are identified both by Ellis (2002) and Leahy (2007). These help me understand my vulnerability to experiencing an unhelpful counter-transference response, for instance a need for approval, intolerance and emotional inhibition. If I am to acknowledge anti-therapeutic reactions to my clients and the dysfunctional schemas underlying them, self-compassion, self-acceptance and humility are important. I have learned that I will neither deal constructively with such counter-transference reactions nor even admit their existence if I am ashamed of having them, especially if I have dysfunctional schemas about being a therapist (for instance, 'I am an experienced therapist and therefore should not have negative reactions to my clients'). To deal with these counter-transference reactions I first need to address any shame-based attitudes towards having such reactions before I consider the issues lying behind the reactions themselves.

In addressing transference and counter-transference issues in therapy, while I am first guided by REBT and CBT theory I am open to other theoretical perspectives if they prove to be more helpful. For this reason I value and undertake continuing professional development issues both within and outside CBT.[6]

In Chapter 3, I will examine the aspect of the working alliance that I have called 'views'. This aspect refers to the understandings that my client and I have on issues pertinent to our shared work in therapy.

Chapter 3

Shared views in therapy

I added the 'views' component of the working alliance (see Dryden, 2006, 2011b) because I considered that Bordin's tripartite component model of the alliance – 'bonds', 'goals' and 'tasks' – did not cover the views (or understandings) that both therapist and client have of salient therapeutic issues.

3.1 The importance of explicit communication in FCBT

In my opinion, effective therapy is based on a set of shared views (or agreed understandings) between my client and myself on a range of issues. Should we disagree on any aspect of the process, we need to identify, explore and resolve the potential obstacle to the client's progress that exists. In view of this potential for disagreement, I am explicit about my views and I encourage my clients to be explicit about theirs. In supervising therapists, my experience has indicated that many problems in therapy could be avoided if therapist and client are clear with each other on whatever issue caused them a problem.

If my client and I disagree on a particular topic then either one of us can refer the issue to the reflection process that I discussed in Chapter 2. If the views on which we differ cannot be reconciled and if this makes therapy non-viable, then this decision has at least been made based on an explicit exchange of opinion and information.

3.2 Negotiated consent

'Negotiated consent' is a term I use to characterise the heart of the views component of the working alliance. I prefer this to the more generally used term 'informed consent' because it reflects the greater reality that my client and I are negotiating important elements of the contract between us.

The term 'informed consent', on the other hand, signifies that the client is informed by me, the therapist, about relevant aspects of my therapy practice and gives their consent to proceed with therapy, based on being so informed. It seems to me that this one-way process does not enable me to be informed by what my client wants so that I can decide whether there are any elements with which I disagree and about which I want to negotiate. It is on the basis of this discussion and negotiation that I can choose to give my consent to proceed or otherwise. For this reason the term 'negotiated consent' reflects more accurately the flexible, pluralistic nature of my practice where the client's views are taken very seriously and they are considered to be an equal partner in the therapy process. If, from the client's perspective, consent cannot be negotiated, they cannot be said to have agreed to the process and thus therapy should not proceed.

What I and my client negotiate about before we both give our consent to proceed is as follows:

- eliciting from the client what therapeutic approach they are seeking and explaining the way I work;
- therapy practicalities;
- confidentiality and its limits;
- contributions of both client and therapist to therapy;
- how both client and therapist conceptualise the problem(s);
- how both client and therapist plan to address the problem(s).

I will deal with each of these issues in this chapter, but first let me make an important point about client roles, which are relevant to the consent process.

3.2.1 Client roles and the consent process

The distinction between 'applicant' and 'client' in interpersonal social work has been pointed out by Seabury, Seabury and Garvin (2011). Drawing on this, I find it useful to add the role of 'enquirer' and to ask myself which of these roles someone occupies when they first make contact with me: are they in the 'enquirer' or 'applicant' role? It should be noted that when a person first makes contact they cannot be in the 'client' role as they have not yet given their consent to anything.

I will now explain a little more about each role.

3.2.1.1 The enquirer role

Being in the 'enquirer' role means that someone is making enquiries about therapy. In this regard, even if they have little idea of what they are

20 Shared views in therapy

seeking, they may be hoping that their initial enquiries will prompt their thinking. Conversely, they may have a clear notion of the kind of therapy they are seeking, but are 'shopping around' for a particular therapist or therapy – and at the right price if they are looking for a therapy in the private sector. Those in the enquirer role make contact by phone or email and I consider it important to spend a little time with them to help them with their enquiries. When an enquirer makes an appointment to see me they can then be said to occupy the 'applicant' role. Also, when a person initially seeks an appointment, but hasn't yet made one, they are also in the 'applicant' role.

3.2.1.2 The applicant role

If someone is in the 'applicant' role they have decided to look for therapy and to seek it from me. Although they may have also made an appointment with me, they do not yet know what working with me might involve, while I don't know whether I am the best person to help the client or whether I can help the client.

3.2.1.3 The client role

By the time someone looking for my help has become a client, we have agreed the following:

- that the way I work (which I refer to here as FCBT) is suitable for that person and that they think this approach could be helpful to them (with the person themselves suggesting modifications);
- that we both think I can potentially help the person;
- that we both understand and agree to fulfil our respective roles and responsibilities;
- that we are both in accord regarding the practicalities of therapy.

At this stage, both of us having negotiated and consented to proceed, the person formally becomes my client.

3.3 Discovering which therapeutic approach the client is looking for and explaining how I work (FCBT)

Before I negotiate consent with a client, I do two things regarding therapy approach. I find out what ideas, if any, the client may have about the

Shared views in therapy 21

approach to therapy they are seeking or consider might help them and I explain the main features of how I work. There is no set order in which these two tasks can be undertaken, but I prefer to do the former task first in order to tailor my response to what the client is seeking.

3.3.1 Finding out from the client what therapeutic approach they are seeking

I start by asking my client what approach to therapy they are seeking. If they are seeking cognitive behaviour therapy (CBT), I will respond as follows. First, I strive to find out what they consider CBT to be and why they think it might help them. I will then outline the features of how I work that may be in line with what they are seeking and I strive to show how appropriate aspects of my own approach may allay any reservations they may have about CBT. The following example illustrates this.

Windy: What sort of approach to therapy are you looking for?
Applicant: Well, everyone keeps talking about CBT, so I guess I'm looking for CBT.
Windy: You sound a little hesitant . . .
Applicant: Well, I am a bit, but I do like the practicality of CBT.
Windy: In what sense?
Applicant: Well, it seems to offer specific, practical things that I will be able to use on my own.
Windy: So can you say what makes you hesitant?
Applicant: Well, it sounds like I'm supposed to do what you tell me to do and I don't like that.
Windy: I wouldn't like it either, but I hope the way we practise CBT together won't be at all like that. First, if I make a suggestion it is purely that – a suggestion and not a prescription. We will always talk it through so that you only need to do what we agree you will do. Second, I am interested in your input about what might be helpful, so the CBT process will not be one way. How does that sound?
Applicant: Very reassuring.

What if what the person is looking for is very different from what I have to offer? In this case, it is important for me to be honest about this and refer the person to a therapist who can offer therapeutic help that is more consistent with the person's preferences.

22 Shared views in therapy

3.3.2 Explaining the way I work to a client

Here is an example of how I explained the way I work to a client:

> My approach to therapy is based on a modern interpretation of an old idea. This modern interpretation states that 'People disturb themselves because they hold a set of rigid, extreme attitudes towards what they regard as life's adversities.'
>
> Once they have disturbed themselves they then try to get rid of their disturbed feelings in ways that ultimately serve to maintain their problems. As a practitioner, I will therefore help you to identify, examine and change the rigid, extreme attitudes that I argue underpin your emotional problems and to develop alternative flexible, non-extreme attitudes.
>
> However, the other major aspect of my practice is that I take very seriously my clients' views and opinions about what determines their problems and what they think will be helpful in addressing these problems. So, I see therapy as a fusion between what I have to offer as a therapist and what you have to offer as a client. There will be a lot of discussion between us about how we will address your problems and what you can do between sessions to help yourself. As therapy proceeds, I will help you take increasing responsibility for using the methods we have agreed to use. My ultimate aim is to help you to become your own therapist. As this happens, we will meet less frequently until you feel you can cope on your own.

3.4 The practicalities of therapy

Although it is not specific to the way I work, it is important that my client and I have a shared agreement on a number or practical issues to do with therapy. These include the following.

3.4.1 The length of therapy sessions

While the fact that my sessions last for 50 minutes is something I know, this may not be the case with clients. They may assume that a session lasts for a full hour and think they have been 'short-changed' if I end a session after 50 minutes. So it is important for me to make it quite clear at the outset that sessions last for 50 minutes.

3.4.2 My fee and how it is to be paid

As I work in private practice, I therefore charge a fee. I am not only clear what this fee is at the outset, but I am also explicit about how I expect payment. Although I do not vary the fee, I am more flexible about how payment may be made.

3.4.3 My cancellation policy

I consider it very important that therapists should be quite clear what their cancellation policy is, in case the client thinks they have given the therapist sufficient notice for cancellation when, in fact, they haven't. I suggest that therapists make this clear in writing. My own cancellation policy is as follows: I invoice a client if they don't provide me with 48-hours' notice to cancel their appointment. The only exception to this would be if there was a serious medical emergency for them, or if anyone in their immediate family required hospitalisation. Moreover, if I don't provide them with 48 hours' notice if I need to cancel a session, then they get the next session free. Again, the only exception to this would be if I, or one of my immediate family, have a serious medical emergency requiring hospitalisation. Please note the balance and reciprocity of this policy, in the spirit of fairness and pluralism.

3.4.4 Extra-therapy contact

I consider it is important for my client and me to be clear with respect to how (or even if) the client can contact me between sessions for any reason other than to cancel a session or to rearrange an appointment. I am clear about my limits in this regard in that I will not engage with them between sessions other than as previously agreed. When a therapist fails to be clear on this issue, a client may end up sending the therapist frequent emails between sessions expecting a response, which is a situation that some therapists may not appreciate. So again, explicitness and agreement are vital here, as elsewhere.

I wish to stress again that according to the way I work, I encourage clients not only to suggest modifications to my practicalities, but also to suggest their own practicalities. The reflection process is at the centre of all the issues between the client and me and if we disagree on any of the practicalities, then these disagreements will need to be resolved before therapy can begin. If not it cannot be said that my client and I have given negotiated consent to proceed.

3.5 Confidentiality and its limits

Although therapy is a confidential process, absolute confidentiality has its limits, which I will make clear to the client. In addition, the client needs to have input into any resultant discussion before we can both give negotiated consent on this issue. The following are the exceptions to absolute confidentiality:

1   If the client poses a significant risk to their own life and will not take steps on their own behalf to protect themselves I will inform a relevant third party.
2   If a third person's client poses a significant risk to the life or well-being (especially in the case where minors are involved) of another person or other people, I will inform that third person and/or the relevant authorities.
3   In cases of past, present or planned episodes of sexual abuse and exploitation, I will inform the appropriate authorities concerning child protection.
4   If a private insurance company is paying for the client's therapy, this company may ask me to provide them with periodic reports of the client's progress and what interventions I have made and/or plan to make in cases where payment is to be renewed.
5   It may be possible for other people to listen to any digital voice recordings of therapy sessions I may make. I therefore need to make it clear to the client who will listen to the recordings and why, including what will be done with them after they have been listened to. I also need to stress that these recordings will only be made if the client provides their written consent. If this consent is not given I will not withhold therapy.
6   If the client persistently and unreasonably refuses to pay my rightful fees I will take appropriate legal steps to recover them.
7   On proper request from the courts or from another legal authority I am legally required to provide notes regarding therapy sessions.

I will provide my clients with a written outline of information about how I work, the practicalities of counselling, the limits to absolute confidentiality and other relevant information. I also require them to sign a form to indicate negotiated consent, which will be referred to as the 'counselling contract'.

3.6 The contributions of therapist and client to FCBT

A key feature of therapy is that client and therapist form a good working alliance. My client and I both have roles and responsibilities to carry out

Shared views in therapy 25

in order to harness the power of this alliance for the client's benefit. It is important to this end that we both understand what our respective contributions are to the process of therapy and agree to make them.

3.6.1 The client's contribution to therapy

By understanding that they have an active part to play in the process the client contributes to the success of therapy and agrees to do the following.

3.6.1.1 Be honest

It is important for the client to be honest with me about the nature of the problem(s) for which they are seeking help. It may be difficult for them to be honest right from the beginning because of the nature of the client's problem(s) and difficulties, and their honesty will in part be facilitated by their experience of my being a trustworthy and understanding source of help.

Client honesty involves not only the client revealing problems, but being open about what they think may or may not be helpful about addressing their problems. They should also provide sincere feedback to me about what they find useful and perhaps not so useful regarding my contribution to therapy. In this respect, the client should refer appropriate matters to the reflection process when necessary.

3.6.1.2 Set goals

Having disclosed their problems, the client needs with my help to set goals, since therapy is a purposeful activity. I will discuss this issue more fully in Chapter 4.

3.6.1.3 Be open to the therapist's input

The client needs to be open both to the points I make and the frameworks I use. The client should adopt a healthy questioning approach to accompany this openness and they should give their honest views, as I have noted above. Ideally, the client should neither accept what I say uncritically, nor reject it immediately if it does not seem to fit with what they are looking for.

3.6.1.4 Carry out negotiated tasks

However skilled I may be as a therapist, unless the client agrees to carry out negotiated tasks to further their goals, they will gain little enduring

26 Shared views in therapy

benefit from therapy. Perhaps this is the client's most important contribution to therapy. They may, of course, experience problems in implementing these tasks and in that case they will need to be honest about these problems with me.

3.6.1.5 Take responsibility for their contributions to the practicalities of therapy

Taking such responsibility involves, for instance, keeping appointments, paying fees in a timely fashion and respecting and abiding by my cancellation policy.

3.6.2 The therapist's contribution to therapy

My contribution to therapy, apart from the professional responsibility to abide by the ethical standards of my professional association, is indicated by the following points, about which the client needs to be informed. They should also contribute a discussion about these points if they have any issues to raise.

3.6.2.1 Safeguard the client's well-being

Ensuring that the person's well-being is safeguarded when they make contact and formally agree to become a client (see above) is my first responsibility. That means not just protecting client confidentiality (see above), but also that I establish a safe place to allow the client to disclose the nature of their problem(s). In addition, I make sure that clients can protect themselves if they are exposed to a significant threat to their well-being either posed by themselves or by another person (or persons). I will take steps to establish suitable protection if the client cannot be protected from such a threat.

3.6.2.2 My contribution facilitates the client's contribution

The following is a summary of my parallel contribution regarding clients' contribution. I endeavour to:

- encourage clients to express their honest views regarding their problem(s), possible ways of addressing these problem(s) and any other matters concerning their therapy, referring any matters that need discussion to the reflection process where appropriate;

- help clients to set meaningful goals (see next chapter);
- show clients that I value their expressing their views in respect to the understanding and addressing of their problem(s) and other relevant therapeutic matters and that I take their views very seriously; I will strive to identify clients' previous successful attempts to deal with similar problems and will integrate these into therapy where appropriate;
- encourage clients to execute their tasks, help them anticipate and deal with (1) potential obstacles to carrying them out and (2) any actual obstacles they may encounter;
- refer any issues to do with therapy practicalities to the reflection process for discussion and resolution.

3.7 How the client and I conceptualise the client's problem(s)

It is important that I develop with the client a shared conceptualisation of the client's problem(s) in order for both of us to be able to discuss ways of addressing them. As I mentioned in the preface, my way of working, which in this book is called FCBT, is a fusion of what both I and the client have to contribute to the process. During the stage of problem conceptualisation, my aim is to agree with the client regarding which problem we are both going to tackle first (assuming the client has more than one problem) and offer the client the ABC framework (given in the Appendix) as an approach to understanding what I term the 'target' problem. I also encourage the client to provide their own conceptualisation of the target problem. Both conceptualisations will explain the factors accounting both for the existence of the problem and for how the problem is maintained. A discussion then follows, in order to establish a shared conceptualisation of the client's problems. I will consider these briefly here, as I will be discussing them in more detail later in the book. Although my conceptualisation will be discussed in this book before that of the client's, this should not necessarily be taken as the preferred order of the way I work. This order is jointly determined by the client and me.

3.7.1 My conceptualisation

When offering my conceptualisation of the client's target problem, I do so by following the ABC model (see the Appendix). This model outlines the factors accounting for both the existence of the problem and its maintenance. As a matter of course, it does not include speculation regarding

28 Shared views in therapy

past origins of the problem. This can also be done as long as I make it clear that these past factors may have contributed to the problem, but have not necessarily caused it.

My conceptualisation is presented as *one* way of understanding this problem rather than *the* way of understanding it. Either I present this framework explicitly and externally – on a whiteboard, for example – or I utilise it internally as a guide to my questions. I will ask my client which approach they favour and having outlined my conceptualisation, I will have a conversation about this with my client before inviting the client to provide their conceptualisation. However, the order of this can be discussed and decided between us.

3.7.2 The client's conceptualisation

It is unlikely that the constructs offered by the client in their conceptualisation of the problem will be expressed in professional language, unless they have been influenced by and have come to use professional ideas. In inviting the client to provide their conceptualisation, I endeavour to help them take the lead in explaining how they see the problem and why it occurs from their perspective. However, I will help them if they falter by asking questions regarding:

- the contexts in which the problem has been experienced;
- the factors accounting for the existence of the problem;
- those factors making the problem better and those factors making it worse.

When eliciting the client's conceptualisation, however, I am *not* as far as possible guided by the ABC model. This will ensure that the client is given the opportunity to provide their conceptualisation in their own way.

There is some interesting research by Barker et al. (1990) on clients' views of their problems and the impact these subsequently may have on therapy. I recommend you look at this research if you are interested in learning more about this issue.

3.7.3 The negotiated conceptualisation

Once the client and I have offered our respective conceptualisations on the client's target problem, our task then is to negotiate a shared conceptualisation. This will form the basis for therapeutic intervention.

My preferred practice is to incorporate the client's view as long as by doing so that is not counterproductive, in my view, for the client. In this case, I would give my client my opinion about why incorporating a certain factor would make things worse for the client rather than helping them. This might include, for instance, a client wanting to incorporate a factor into the shared conceptualisation that will prevent them from addressing the problem in the long term, but might afford relief in the short term (for example, reassurance-seeking). Providing such an explanation is usually enough for the client to agree to omit the factor from the negotiated conceptualisation.

3.7.4 Problem conceptualisation and 'case' conceptualisation

The distinction between problem conceptualisation[1] and case conceptualisation is as follows. Problem conceptualisation (or problem assessment), as shown above, involves my client and me developing a shared understanding of factors explaining a target problem's existence (that is, the problem targeted for change) and why this persists. Case conceptualisation involves taking all the problems the client wants to deal with in therapy and developing an overall shared understanding of the factors that might explain why these problems exist as well as why they persist. It looks for patterns among these problems and aims to explain any differences that may be found.

Imagine you are taking a long car journey involving five overnight stays in hotels in different parts of the country. Planning the whole route before you set off is akin to case conceptualisation while your planning the route to the first hotel is akin to problem conceptualisation. So, according to the way I work, when I adopt a case conceptualisation approach, I will only commence with change-based intervention once a shared conceptualisation has been developed between my client and me. On the other hand, when I take a problem conceptualisation approach, an intervention will be initiated after the target problem is understood, but before the whole terrain has been mapped.

Although I can adopt either approach, I am more likely to adopt a problem conceptualisation approach than a case conceptualisation approach. This is because I tend to develop the latter as therapy proceeds rather than before it starts. In fact, a conceptualisation of the 'case' is often enhanced once therapeutic intervention has been initiated on a target problem, because I can then incorporate the client's response to this intervention into the overall case conceptualisation.

30 Shared views in therapy

When, from a pluralistic point of view, a client looks for help for more than one problem I will outline the two different approaches to conceptualisation and involve the client in a discussion regarding the most productive way forward for them. The working alliance is thus strengthened between us.

3.8 How my client and I plan to address the client's problems

In this chapter I have already pointed out that I outline the way I practise *in general*. The client can therefore make an informed decision about whether they wish to make use of this kind of help. I have also suggested that it is really important to take seriously what the client thinks would be most helpful to them so that we both ensure that these elements are incorporated into the client's therapy.

From what I said to the client in Section 3.3.2 about my way of working, you will note that I was quite explicit about how I conceptualise clients' problems as well as how I approach their amelioration. Indeed, I hope you can see how my statement to the client in Section 3.3.2 regarding my practice followed logically from my statement to the person concerning problem conceptualisation.

At this stage my task is to summarise my perspective on addressing the client's target problem and seeking the client's view on this issue. The order of doing this will again be jointly decided by my client and me. After having expressed these views, my client and I will progress towards a negotiated treatment plan. I will now deal with each of these three steps in more detail.

3.8.1 I outline my approach to the client's target problem

At this point I suggest what my client and I can both do to deal with the client's target problem. Please note that this is a *specific* version of the *general* method of explaining my approach, which I outlined earlier, and is tailored to tackling the client's target problem. I will now discuss broad therapy strategies rather than outlining specific therapy techniques. For instance, I will tell the person that I will help them stand back and question the specific rigid, extreme attitudes underlying their target problem and their alternative flexible, non-extreme attitudes. I will then outline a broad strategy for the client to weaken their conviction in the former and develop their conviction in the latter.

3.8.2 The client outlines what they think will help them address their target problem

When I ask clients to offer their views on what they consider might help them address their target problem effectively, I will at first allow them to express themselves in their own way. Should it be necessary, I will prompt them in the following way:

- What have you tried that made things better in addressing your problem?
- What have you tried that has made no difference?
- What have you done that actually made things worse?
- Have you considered doing anything that you thought might help with the problem, but which so far hasn't done so?
- Have you done anything that was helpful with other problems and which might be helpful with this one?

Having gathered this information, I collate it to form the client's views regarding ways to help them address their target problem.

3.8.3 Towards a negotiated approach to addressing the client's target problem

From the perspective of a working alliance, it is important for my client and me to agree on how we are to approach dealing with the former's problems. We therefore need to view how our respective conceptualisations can be coordinated to form a negotiated treatment approach.

In Chapter 4, I consider the third domain of the working alliance: goals.

Chapter 4

Negotiated and agreed goals in therapy

As pointed out many years ago by Alfred Adler (1927), all human endeavour has a purpose. When, therefore, a client seeks help from me, they have some idea of what they hope to achieve from therapy. Such goals may be stated explicitly or they may have an implicit idea about them, but they do exist and it is important for my client and me to understand what they are. My goals for the client are based on my view of psychological health. I will emphasise in this chapter the importance I attach to the negotiation of client goals between the client and me, as well as of being clear about what they are and agreeing on them.

I begin this chapter by considering how clients typically express their therapeutic goals regarding their target problems and how I am inclined to respond. I will then look at goals related to the target problems from my perspective before finally discussing the negotiation of goals in regard to the client's psychological state.

4.1 The client's perspective on goals with respect to the target problem

I will discuss situations in this section where a client sets a goal or goals, which, if I agree with them as therapist, may prove to be problematic for the therapeutic process. I need to offer the client feedback here as elsewhere, regarding the problematic nature of their goal before negotiating a goal based on this feedback. If the client still wishes to set a goal that may prove problematic for the therapeutic process, I am prepared to accept this goal if it will preserve the working alliance, provided that doing so does not constitute a risk to the client or others. I will encourage the client to review the result of any attempts to reach a goal that proves problematic and will re-negotiate the goal if the client sees that it is problematic or if they admit to being wrong in their initial judgement.

Negotiated and agreed goals in therapy   33

In this section, therefore, I will list the client's problematic goals to show how I would respond before negotiating an agreed goal with the client.

4.1.1 When the client sets a vague goal

Should the client set a vague goal it is important for me to help them make this goal as specific as possible. Here are a few examples of vague goals: 'I want to be happy'; 'I want to get over my anxiety'; and 'I want to get on with my life'. I may use the commonly employed acronym in this situation that represents an antidote to vague goals. The acronym is SMART. Goals that are smart are: Specific, Measurable, Attainable, Realistic and Timely. I use SMART when helping clients to set goals that address disturbance and dissatisfaction and those promoting development.

4.1.2 When the client wants to change 'A'

Rather than changing their unconstructive responses to the adversity at 'A' to those that are constructive, a client may often wish to change 'A' itself – either the situation in which the problem occurs and/or the adversity about which the person has the problem. If this is the case and 'A' can be changed, I help them to understand that the best opportunity they have to change 'A' is when they are in a healthy frame of mind. This may be achieved when their responses to this 'A' are constructive. Therefore, they need to change their disturbed responses at 'C' before they can change 'A'.

4.1.3 When the client wants to change another person

A client's target problem may be centred on their relationship with another person or group of people, and if so their goal may be to change the other(s). In such cases, as therapist I need to help the client see that this goal is inappropriate as the behaviour of others is not under the direct control of the client and they may lead to behavioural change in the other. Attempts to influence others, however, are under the direct control of the client and they *may* lead to behavioural change. They are appropriate goals in such cases. However, in these cases I will help the client to consider their responses when their attempts at influence do not work. It is often important in such cases to help clients deal constructively with these failed attempts. The best time for the client to influence another person for the better, as mentioned earlier, is when they are in a constructive frame of mind rather than a disturbed one. I am faced with

34 Negotiated and agreed goals in therapy

two tasks if, therefore, the client is in a disturbed frame of mind and wishes to change another person. I need first to provide the client with an acceptable rationale for negotiating an 'addressing disturbance' goal. I then need to help the client understand the importance of setting a goal within their control (in other words, their behaviour) rather than outside their control (in other words, the outcome of their behaviour).

4.1.4 When the client nominates a goal based on experiencing less of their problematic response

When I ask a client about their goals in relation to the adversity at 'A', a client may often say that they want to feel less of the disturbed emotion (for example less anxious) that featured in their target problem. Many therapists may accept this as a legitimate goal, but I contend that when a client holds a rigid attitude they take a preference (for instance for acceptance) and make it rigid (e.g. 'I want to be accepted, and therefore I have to be'). When clients hold a flexible attitude, they take the same preference and maintain its flexibility by negating possible rigidity (for instance, I want to be accepted, but it is not necessary that I am). The strength of unhealthy negative emotions in the case of rigid attitudes, and of healthy negative emotions, in the case of flexible attitudes, is determined by the strength of the preference when that preference is not met. Under these circumstances, the stronger the preference the stronger will be the negative emotion of both types. My goal, based on this analysis, is to help the person experience a healthy negative emotion of relative intensity to the unhealthy negative emotion rather than encouraging them to endeavour to experience an unhealthy negative emotion of decreased intensity. Having made this point, I ask the client for their reaction to it and discuss areas of difference before a joint position on the issue is taken.

4.1.5 When the client nominates a goal based on experiencing the absence of the problematic response

When the client nominates the absence of the problem as their goal (for instance, 'I don't want to feel anxious when giving a talk') I am also prepared. If the client says this, I will help them to see that it is impossible to live in a response vacuum and from there, before discussing the issue with the client, I can propose a set of healthy responses to their adversity as their goal.

4.1.6 When the client nominates as a goal a positive response to the situation in which they experienced their problem and bypasses the adversity

When I ask the client for their goal they may also nominate a positive response to the situation in which they experienced the problem while bypassing the adversity. For instance, a client may be anxious about revealing gaps in their knowledge while giving public presentations and will say: 'I want to become confident at giving public presentations.' By so doing they will have bypassed dealing with the actual adversity (namely, revealing gaps in their knowledge). I would ask them in this case how they can become confident at giving public presentations while they are anxious about revealing their ignorance. I help this client to set an appropriate goal with respect to this adversity, as well as helping them take the next step and work towards increasing their confidence about their performance at giving public presentations, after they have dealt constructively with the adversity.

4.1.7 When a client wants to feel indifferent in the face of an adversity

A client may sometimes say that their goal is not to care about a particular adversity when, in reality, they do care about it. Their disturbed feelings, in fact, indicate that they do care. In my practice I help my client to understand what not caring or indifference really means. I might therefore ask them who they would like to win in the Ebac Northern League Division Two football game between Hebburn Town and Ryton & Crawcrook Albion. To this they might reply: 'I don't care.' I would respond to them that this is true indifference, when you truly do not care about two choices. A client, on the other hand, normally does care about whether an adversity exists or not and thus it is not realistic for them to feel indifferent concerning something about which they care.

4.1.8 When a client nominates a goal that is dangerous or unrealistic

A client sometimes nominates a goal, which, in Law and Jacob's (2015) terms, is 'unacceptable'. They mean that this is because the goal is dangerous (e.g. a person with anorexia wanting to set a goal to lose weight, or someone with depression wanting to be helped to end their life), or because a goal is unrealistic (e.g. someone with a physical disability wanting to be a professional footballer).

(Law & Jacob, 2015: 16)

Law and Jacob (2015) add that these goals should not be dismissed but be a prelude for discussion and careful renegotiation. In such cases, I find it particularly helpful to encourage the client to imagine responding to a friend who nominates such goals as this will provide the client with enough distance to enable them to participate in negotiating their own goals with me as their therapist.

4.2 My perspective on goals with respect to the target problem

In contrast to the client's perspective on goals, I will now consider my perspectives on goals.

4.2.1 Focus on the target problem

Suppose my client and I have decided to target one of the former's problems for therapeutic help. This, as we have seen, is called the 'target problem'. In assessing this target problem, I need to understand, if possible, both a specific example of the target problem and its general nature.

4.2.1.1 The situationally based AC problem focus

Having selected a target problem and put it in its general and specific context, it is necessary to engage with the client in the process of understanding the nature of the problem. In doing so, I use the 'A' and 'C' components of the 'ABC' framework of psychological disturbance that I employ in my work (see the Appendix). We have already seen that 'A' stands for Adversity and this occurs in a situational context. The emotional, behavioural and cognitive responses to the adversity at 'A' are known as 'C', while basic attitudes, which we don't need to know about for the purposes of the goal-setting process, are known as 'B'.

For example, Paul is anxious about an upcoming date and is particularly so about revealing his social awkwardness. The behavioural features of his anxiety consist of over-rehearsing the things he plans to discuss with his date and drinking too much. The cognitive features of this anxiety consist of fearing that the woman will regard him as strange

Negotiated and agreed goals in therapy   37

and will tell all her friends he is weird. According to the ABC framework, this will appear as:

Paul's problem

Situation	= Going on a date
A (Adversity)	= Revealing my social awkwardness
B (Basic attitudes: Rigid and Extreme)	= Not known
C (Consequences) (emotional)	= Anxiety
(behavioural)	= Over-rehearsing topic for discussion before the date
	= Drinking too much during the date
(cognitive)	= 'The woman will think I am strange.'
	= 'She will tell all her friends that I am weird.'

4.2.2 Focus on goals

Having helped myself and the client to understand the 'A' (Adversity) and 'C' (Consequences) components of the latter's target problem and the situation in which this problem takes place, I am now in a good position to help the client set a goal regarding that problem. Questions I might ask to initiate this process include the following:

- 'At the end of therapy what would you take away with you that would give you a sense that you could effectively deal with the issue?'
- 'How would you like to be able to deal with the situation or adversity rather than responding to it by [name here the client's current problematic response]?'
- 'Rather than responding to the situation or adversity by [name here the client's current problematic response] what would you consider as your acceptable constructive response?'

4.2.2.1 The importance of negotiating a goal in response to the adversity rather than in response to the situation

When people discuss their problems in therapy they frequently talk about their disturbed responses to situations they find problematic. So, when Paul first told me the area he wanted to focus on in his therapy he spoke about his anxiety about going on dates. When we both looked at this in more detail, we found that what Paul was most anxious about regarding going on dates was to reveal his social awkwardness to the woman he

38 Negotiated and agreed goals in therapy

was meeting. Going on dates, then, in the ABC framework was the situation in which Paul felt anxious and his adversity was revealing his social awkwardness.

If clients are inclined to identify situations in nominating their target problem, they will do the same in discussing their goal unless guided to set a goal with respect to their adversity. In such cases, I offer them a rationale for providing this guidance. The client needs to accept this rationale before we both proceed. I might therefore ask the client: 'Do you think it would be more useful if I helped you to deal with dates more productively or with the possibility that you might reveal your social awkwardness on these dates?' Or I might ask 'Do you think I can help you best with going on dates if you are anxious about revealing your social awkwardness or if you are concerned, but not anxious, about this?'

4.2.2.2 The importance of assuming temporarily that the client's adversity is accurate

When clients come to therapy and are struggling in the face of an adversity, I provide them with an opportunity to deal constructively with that adversity. In some forms of therapy, the emphasis may be on helping clients to realise that their inferred adversities at 'A' are distorted (e.g. 'my boss wants to see me because he wants to tell me off') and the emphasis will be on helping them by questioning such distorted inferences. Although this stance is often useful, it does not necessarily help the client to deal constructively with adversity from their point of view. Moreover, it is possible that they may encounter situations where their inferences prove correct. Thus, although Paul may distort reality sometimes by assuming he has revealed his social awkwardness on dates when in fact he hasn't, he may in fact do so and it is therefore important that I help him deal with this possibility, assuming that he sees the sense of doing so.

By encouraging my client to deal with the adversity from their frame of reference and therefore to set goals for dealing constructively with it, I find it is useful to ask them to assume for the time being that they are accurate in inferring the presence of the adversity. The best time for clients to review the accuracy or otherwise of their adversity inference is when they are not in a disturbed frame of mind about such an inference, namely when they have achieved their goal of dealing constructively with the adversity. The client who therefore thinks the reason their boss wants to see them is to criticise them is in a better position to consider the accuracy of this inference if they are concerned but not anxious about this inference than if they are anxious about it.

4.2.2.3 Helping my client to construct healthy responses to the adversity as goals

After the client has understood the importance of negotiating a goal in relation to facing their adversity, my next task is to help them develop healthy responses to that adversity. These will serve as their goals relating to their target problem. The best way for me to do this, in my view, is to look at the situationally based AC components that they identified when seeking to understand the problem. The person was most disturbed about the 'A' component, namely the adversity in a situationally based context. It is important in negotiating a goal with the client that they retain this same 'A' component. If they do not, they will not be helped to deal with their adversity constructively. The emotional, behavioural and cognitive responses to the adversity are the 'C' components. In helping a client to develop healthy responses, I need ideally to help them identify healthy responses that are alternatives to each of the unhealthy responses in the three response categories listed above, namely emotional, behavioural and cognitive.

4.2.2.3.1 HEALTHY EMOTIONAL RESPONSES AS GOALS

A person who has a problem with an adversity will usually experience a negative emotion. I term this negative emotion in my work 'unhealthy' when it leads the person to get stuck, or when it is associated with a range of unconstructive behavioural and cognitive responses discouraging the person from facing up to the adversity and dealing with it constructively. When the client responds constructively to this adversity they will also experience a negative emotion. This is because the 'A' is negative and feeling negative when something negative happens is healthy. I again refer in my work to this negative emotion as 'healthy' when it allows the client to get unstuck, or is associated with a variety of constructive behavioural and cognitive responses and when it encourages the client to face up to the adversity and deal constructively with it.

In my experience I have found that clients can find negotiating a healthy emotional response to an adversity quite difficult since people generally assume that such a response involves the reduction or absence of an unhealthy negative emotion rather than the presence of a healthy negative emotion (as described above). In addition, we do not have terms in the English language to denote healthy negative emotions in a way that clearly differentiate them from unhealthy negative emotions. Consequently, it is important to negotiate terms with the client for both the unhealthy negative emotion experienced in their target problem and the healthy negative emotion they will experience should they reach their goal.

4.2.2.3.2 HEALTHY BEHAVIOURAL RESPONSES AS GOALS

The easiest healthy responses to construct are perhaps behavioural in nature. In this respect it is important that I help the person, if possible, to name the presence of a healthy behaviour rather than the absence of an unhealthy behaviour.

4.2.2.3.3 HEALTHY COGNITIVE RESPONSES AS GOALS

In constructing healthy cognitive responses to the adversity, that is, responses accompanying emotions at 'C', I find the following a useful rule of thumb: healthy cognitive responses will be balanced and will incorporate negative, neutral and positive features of the situationally based 'A' (for instance 'The woman may think I am strange, but she may not and may even find me interesting. She may tell her friends I am weird, but again she may not and she may tell them she had a good time'), whereas unhealthy cognitive responses are highly distorted and skewed to the negative (e.g. 'The woman will think I am strange. She will tell all her friends that I am weird').

Paul, who we met above, used the ABC framework and was thus helped to set the following goals:

Paul's goal

Situation	= Going on a date
A (Adversity)	= Revealing my social awkwardness
B (Basic attitudes: Flexible and Non-Extreme)	= Not known
C (Consequences as goals)	
(emotional)	= Concern
(behavioural)	= Spending 10 minutes before the date making notes of what to say, but without over-rehearsing the topics
	= Drinking one alcoholic drink on the date
(cognitive)	= 'The woman may think I am strange, but she may not and she may even find me interesting.'
	= 'She may tell her friends that I am weird, but again she may not and she may even tell them she had a good time.'

4.3 Negotiating goals appropriate to the client's psychological state

I tend to be called upon to negotiate three types of goals: 'addressing disturbance' goals (as discussed above), 'addressing dissatisfaction' goals and 'addressing development' goals. I will revisit 'addressing disturbance' goals and then discuss the other two sets of goals. It is important from a working alliance perspective that (1) my client and I address goals relevant to the former's psychological state and (2) that we are in agreement concerning goals, as mentioned at the outset.

4.3.1 Negotiating 'addressing disturbance' goals

My message so far in this chapter has been that when clients are psychologically disturbed about adversities it is important for me to help them address such a disturbance and to set goals reflecting the fact that it is healthy to feel badly (but not disturbed) about the adversity and, in fact, doing this helps them face and deal with the adversity. The emotional components of this disturbance are called 'unhealthy negative emotions', while the emotional components of their healthy emotional counterparts are referred to as 'healthy negative emotions'. An alternative way of considering this is that where unhealthy negative emotions represent 'disturbance', healthy negative emotions represent 'dissatisfaction', and these realistic negative psychological states are free from disturbance. I have already pointed out that we do not have an agreed common language for healthy negative emotions. However, bearing this in mind, Table 4.1 summarises common adversities, the unhealthy negative emotions or disturbance for which people seek help and the healthy negative emotions or dissatisfaction forming realistic emotional goals in the face of adversity.

I frequently summarise this position with clients by stating that I can help them feel badly regarding the adversities they face. When they object saying they are already feeling badly, I point out that they are actually feeling disturbed about the adversity and while I can help them remove the disturbance, I can't help them remove their bad feelings, which are, as I point out, a realistic, healthy response to adversity! I frequently find it valuable to 'unpack' the difference between unhealthy negative emotions (disturbance) and healthy negative emotions (dissatisfaction) by distinguishing between their behavioural and cognitive referents.

42 Negotiated and agreed goals in therapy

Table 4.1 Common adversities, unhealthy negative emotions or disturbance (problems) and healthy negative emotions or dissatisfaction (goals)

Adversity	Unhealthy negative emotions (disturbance): problem	Healthy negative emotions (dissatisfaction): goal
• Threat	Anxiety	Concern
• Loss • Failure • Undeserved plight (self or other)	Depression	Sadness
• Moral code violation • Hurting others	Guilt	Remorse
• Falling very short of ideal • Others negatively evaluate self	Shame	Disappointment
• Self more invested in relationship than is the other • Relationship rule violation (other treats self badly and undeservedly)	Hurt	Sorrow
• Rule violation • Threat to self-esteem • Frustration	Unhealthy anger	Healthy anger
• Other poses threat to one's relationship	Unhealthy jealousy	Healthy jealousy
• Other has something that self prizes but does not have	Unhealthy envy	Healthy envy

When clients have achieved their 'addressing disturbance' goals and are then healthily dissatisfied about their adversities, they are ready to set goals addressing their dissatisfied psychological state.

4.3.2 Negotiating 'addressing dissatisfaction' goals

It is useful in thinking about helping clients to set 'addressing dissatisfaction' goals to consider the Serenity Prayer attributed to Reinhold Niebuhr: 'God, grant me the serenity to accept the things I cannot change, the courage to change the things I can, and the wisdom to know the difference' (Narcotics Anonymous, 1976). The following 'addressing dissatisfaction' goals are relevant.

Negotiated and agreed goals in therapy   43

4.3.2.1 Goals that relate to the probable existence of the adversity

In the case example given above, Paul was anxious about revealing his social awkwardness on a date. As we have discussed, this was his adversity at 'A'. Once Paul achieves the dissatisfied psychological state of being concerned rather than the disturbed psychological state of being anxious, he can stand back to consider the accuracy of his prediction, namely that he will reveal his social awkwardness. The end result of this process is that Paul should be in a position to come to a conclusion on the 'inference accuracy' question. I am guided in my work in this area by the idea that the client's judgement is best informed by the 'best bet' (as the concept is known in the field of perceptual psychology) or as it is termed in philosophy the 'inference to the best explanation' (Lipton, 2004). I therefore encourage clients to assume that an inference of adversity is probably true if it provides the best explanation of the available data. If it does not, I encourage them to develop and accept as probably true an alternative inference. The client's inference of adversity quite often does not fit the available data, in which case it can be rejected. When the client does this, they lose their dissatisfaction because they no longer think that the adversity exists.

4.3.2.2 Goals that seek to change the adversity (if it can be changed)

Assuming that the inference of adversity has been accepted as probably true (for instance, it is probably true that Paul will reveal his social awkwardness), I can then help the client set goals designed to change this adversity. As I have found, it is important to take care here as an important distinction needs to be made between goals representing the client's enactment of behaviour designed to bring about change in the adversity that is under the client's control (in Paul's case this involves practising talking to women on dates) and the change or otherwise itself, which is not under the client's direct control. I will encourage clients to set the former goal rather than the latter.

Behaviour designed to change an adversity is carried out best when the client is in a dissatisfied psychological state rather than in a disturbed psychological state, and I am guided by this principle.

4.3.2.3 Goals that seek to change the situation in which the adversity occurs (if it can be changed)

I distinguished earlier in the chapter between an adversity (what the client is most disturbed about in a situation) and the situation in which

44 Negotiated and agreed goals in therapy

the adversity occurs. For instance, a client who has not been invited to a work meeting (situation) infers from this that he is not liked at work (adversity). I bear this notion in mind when I help a client set a goal designed to change the *situation* in which the adversity occurs, assuming it can be changed – for instance when I help a client set a goal designed to change the *adversity* (as above). I again encourage the client to set enactment of a change-directed behaviour as a goal rather than as the effect of that behaviour. I will therefore encourage the client to approach the person responsible for sending out invitations to the meeting in order to get an invitation, although whether they actually receive one is out of their control.

4.3.2.4 Relevant goals when the adversity and/or situation cannot be changed

When the adversity and/or the situation in which it occurred cannot be changed or when the client's efforts to change them have not been successful, I remind myself that at this point the client is in a dissatisfied rather than disturbed psychological state of mind. Therefore the worst case scenario is that I can help the client to live with the adversity while remaining in a dissatisfied psychological state of mind during those times when they cannot help but focus on the situation/adversity. On the other hand, I also have other options here. I can, for instance, help the client to set the following goals:

- to avoid the situation/adversity as much as possible but to remain in the environment;
- as long as it does not impact negatively on the client's life to change the environment and move away from the situation/adversity;
- in order for the client not to dwell on the adversity, to develop mindfulness skills;
- even though the situation/adversity continues to exist, to act in ways consistent with one's values.

4.3.3 Negotiating 'promoting development' goals

Having helped the client achieve their 'addressing disturbance' goals and their 'addressing dissatisfaction' goals, I am now able to help them achieve goals relating to their growth or development. These are called 'life goals' by Mackrill (2011). Such goals are designed to help clients get more out of their work, relationships and life in general. The more specific they are, the more likely is it that they will be pursued and therefore achieved, although it is possible that these goals may be process-related in nature, that is, goals involving the achievement and continuation of behaviour (e.g. to jog for one hour a day, six days a week) rather than involving a definite end-point. It is fair to say that the way the field has developed, addressing disturbance and dissatisfaction goals is considered to be mainly the province of psychotherapy and counselling (which are the focus of this text). Promoting development goals is considered largely the province of coaching (which is the focus of Dryden, 2018).

I will discuss in Chapter 5 the final component of the working alliance – tasks.

Chapter 5

Goal-directed tasks in therapy

Activities carried out by my client and me that are goal-directed in nature are called 'tasks'. They can either be broad or specific; however, the key thing to remember is that because of the flexible, pluralistic nature of my approach to therapy, both my tasks as therapist and my client's tasks are negotiated before being agreed. Many books on CBT describe a plethora of tasks (see Leahy, 2017) and I will focus later in this book on tasks that concentrate on working with attitudes as this is at the heart of how I work (see Chapters 7 and 8).

5.1 Using working alliance theory to inform the selection and use of therapeutic tasks

I will consider in this chapter therapeutic tasks from a working alliance perspective and will discuss how, when working with the client to select and implement such tasks, I draw upon this perspective.

5.1.1 Helping the client to understand that they have therapeutic tasks to perform and what these tasks are likely to be

For some people therapy tends to have an aura of mystery about it. However, for therapy to be effective in practice, the client needs to do more than just turn up every week and talk. Instead they need to engage in some 'work'. Unless the client accepts and implements the principle of 'working for change', the gains they are likely to achieve from working with me may well be superficial and ephemeral. From this it follows that if they are truly to be helped one of my tasks is to encourage clients to adopt and implement a 'work to change' philosophy.

If a client either explicitly or implicitly does not understand (a) that they need to perform tasks in the therapeutic process and (b) what these tasks are broadly speaking, then their progress through the therapeutic process faces a potential obstacle. This may be dealt with, as with other potential obstacles, by referring the matter for discussion to that part of the therapy dialogue that I call 'the reflection process' where my client and I take a step back to discuss what has gone on between us during therapy sessions (see Chapter 2).

5.1.2 Engaging the client in a discussion about the selection of therapeutic tasks

After the client has accepted the need to perform tasks in FCBT we next need to discuss what these tasks should be. In selecting the client's therapeutic tasks, possibly the most important point is that this process should be done jointly. I am guided about client tasks from the research and professional literatures regarding what tasks have been shown to be effective for the type of problem for which the client is seeking help, while the client is guided in their suggestions about their own tasks from their own experience of what has previously worked for them and what they think might work for them in the future.

Client task selection is not, according to the way in which I work, a matter of my making a task suggestion, providing a rationale for its use and then the client accepting the rationale. Instead, I convey the idea that task selection involves the pooling of our resources, with both of us offering suggestions, discussing them and then making a decision based on our discussion.

5.1.3 Negotiating my tasks as therapist

I have tasks to perform as well during the therapy process and I need to make these clear to my client. These tasks are again likely to be derived from the professional literature. I will suggest from a pluralistic perspective the use of tasks that come both from within the broad field of CBT (see Leahy, 2017) and from other therapy approaches (see e.g. Kellogg, 2015). I will then invite my client to give feedback on my tasks as therapist.

A hallmark of pluralism within psychotherapy is that, at this stage, I invite the client to suggest therapist tasks that they might consider to be helpful to them. For example, it is likely that other people have been helpful to the client not just with respect to their target problem, but

48 Goal-directed tasks in therapy

generally, and I will seek this information and initiate a discussion with the client regarding what I can do to utilise these helpful contributions from the client's past.

5.1.4 Helping the client see that performing their agreed tasks will help them to achieve their goals

Although a client may understand what their tasks are and agree to carry them out, they may be uncertain how carrying these out may actually help them achieve their goals. From an alliance perspective, therefore, it is very important that I help the client to understand the connection between carrying out their tasks and achieving their goals. This applies whether the client's tasks are carried out within the therapy session or between therapy sessions in their everyday lives.

5.1.5 Ensuring that the client has the capability to carry out the suggested therapeutic tasks before agreeing them

For the purpose of engaging in therapy tasks, clients need to be able to perform these tasks. However, not all clients will be capable of engaging in Socratic questioning when this is used in therapy (that is, questioning designed to help a client to reflect on their own thinking and attitudes without the therapist – namely, myself – making suggestions or offering my own opinions). Without being capable of engaging in certain therapy tasks means that no amount of training in the use of these tasks will be of use to the client. In sharp contrast, there are situations where a client may have the capability but not the necessary *skills* to perform these tasks. In such cases they will benefit from training and/or instructions regarding the necessary skills and how to use them.

It is sometimes relatively easy to detect that a client is not capable of engaging in certain therapy tasks. For instance, a task may require a relatively high degree of intellectual intelligence, which it may be clear to me that a particular client just does not have. In the majority of cases, though, it is less clear whether or not a client has the required capability. In these cases, the best way of determining this is through trial and error. If the client still cannot engage in the task, after a reasonable number of attempts to encourage them to use a particular task and after appropriate training in task-relevant skills, it is reasonable to conclude that they do not have the necessary task-related capability. I endeavour to decide this in a way that does not demoralise the client. It helps if I have encouraged

Goal-directed tasks in therapy   49

them to see that one of my tasks as therapist is to identify and suggest appropriate tasks for them – a procedure involving trial and error. I also emphasise that different clients bring different capabilities to therapy, and that effective therapy involves matching particular client capabilities to therapy tasks. If a client should become disturbed about their lack of a relevant capability after I have taken the appropriate steps to minimise such distress, their reaction may well reflect one of their problems. In such cases I will invite them to put this issue on the therapeutic agenda.

5.1.6 Ensuring that a client has the necessary skills to carry out the suggested therapeutic tasks before agreeing them

As mentioned above, skills are different from capabilities. A client may be capable of engaging in a process of examining their rigid, extreme attitudes, for instance, but may not know how to do this. After they have been taught these skills they are able to give expression to their capability. Thus, although executing particular tasks may help clients to change, if my client does not have the necessary skills in their repertoire to carry these out, this poses a threat to the working alliance in the task domain.

It may therefore be productive for me to train the client to execute their negotiated and agreed tasks if they lack the necessary skills to do so at a given point. For instance, the following skills are involved in the client task of engaging in a dialectical examination of their rigid, extreme attitudes in FCBT:

1   becoming aware of feeling emotionally disturbed and/or of acting in a self-defeating manner;
2   identifying one or more rigid, extreme attitudes underpinning such disturbance;
3   formulating flexible, non-extreme alternative attitudes;
4   standing back and examining these two sets of attitudes for their empirical, logical and pragmatic value for the client in addressing their problem; it should be clear from such a detailed analysis of client task behaviour that the client's ability to execute such a task successfully depends upon:

    (a) how effective I have been in training the client to do this within therapy sessions; and
    (b) how much successful practice the client has engaged in both within and between therapy sessions.

50 Goal-directed tasks in therapy

5.1.7 Helping the client to develop the confidence to execute the relevant tasks

A similar point can be made here as above. Certain client tasks (in particular the so-called 'homework tasks' that clients are asked to do between sessions) require a certain degree of task confidence on the part of the client if they are to be executed successfully. The client may therefore understand the nature of the task, see its therapeutic relevance, have the ability and skills to carry it out, but may still not do so because they fear that they don't have the confidence. Should this be the case, I can then prepare the client in one of two ways. First, I may need to help the client practise the tasks in controlled conditions (usually within therapy sessions) so that that they feel sufficiently confident to do the agreed tasks independently. Second, I may encourage the client to carry out the tasks unconfidently, pointing out that confidence arises from the result of undertaking an activity (that is, from practice) and is rarely experienced before the activity is first attempted. I may use an analogy that is within the experience of clients themselves (for example, learning to drive a car) to help them understand this important point.

5.1.8 Ensuring that the task has sufficient therapeutic potency to facilitate goal achievement

If all the above-mentioned conditions have been met (i.e. the client understands the nature and therapeutic relevance of task execution, and they have enough ability, skills and confidence to perform the relevant tasks), the client may still not gain therapeutic benefit from undertaking the tasks because they may not be sufficiently powerful therapeutically to help them achieve their goals. For instance, certain client tasks, if carried out well enough, will probably lead to client change. Therefore, if clients expose themselves either in reality or via the imagination, to a phobic object, this may well yield some therapeutic benefit (Rachman and Wilson, 1980). Certain tasks may have much less therapeutic potency, though, to achieve a similar result. For instance, it has still to be demonstrated that examining one's rigid, extreme attitudes in the consulting room alone as opposed to in the feared situation has much therapeutic effect in overcoming phobias. It is important that I keep abreast of the current research literature on the subject at hand and that I do not discourage the client by asking them to carry out unlikely tasks, even under the most favourable conditions, to produce much therapeutic benefit.

Regarding this there are certain client problems that do seem to call for the execution of specific client tasks. Apart from phobic problems as mentioned above, obsessive-compulsive problems seem to require the client to employ some variant of response prevention in their everyday life (Emmelkamp, 2013) and problems of depression seem to require the client to become active, modify distorted thought patterns (Hollon & Beck, 2013) and improve problematic elements in their significant interpersonal relationships (Cuipers et al., 2011) for the purpose of gaining therapeutic benefit. In Britain, the National Institute of Health and Care Excellence (NICE) publishes up-to-date guidelines that outline which therapies are likely to be effective for a range of client problems, although on the whole performing a wide variety of tasks may yield a comparable therapeutic result (Stiles et al., 1986; Wampold & Imel, 2015).

5.1.9 Guarding against the use of tasks that unwittingly serve to perpetuate the client's problems

It is necessary to be aware that what I do in the consultation room and what the client does inside and outside that room may unwittingly serve to perpetuate the client's problems rather than helping them deal effectively with them. First, the client may, at their own suggestion, do various things that, while being designed to help them overcome their problems, have the opposite effect. Many anxious clients thus seek to avoid anxiety-provoking situations before getting anxious, or withdraw from these situations when they get anxious, in an attempt to deal with these anxious feelings. This behaviour prevents clients from facing their fears and dealing appropriately with them and they therefore remain anxious in the long run.

Some therapists respond to their clients' anxieties by giving inappropriate reassurance and suggestions that their clients distract themselves when they feel anxious. In the first case, reassurance is often ineffective because anxious clients are often not reassurable. In the second case, distraction is a form of withdrawal and, as a result, clients again do not face their fears armed appropriately with coping strategies. I will implement neither of these strategies and generally I think carefully about the problem perpetuation implications of what I say and do in therapy. I will, again, discuss this issue with the client and encourage their input on the matter.

52 Goal-directed tasks in therapy

5.1.10 Ensuring that the client is in a sufficiently good frame of mind to execute their tasks

I have so far outlined some of the favourable conditions that need to exist if clients are to get the most out of therapy in the task domain. However favourable these conditions are, clients need to be in a sufficiently good frame of mind to capitalise on them. If the client is very anxious, for example, they will probably be unable to implement tasks involving much focused attention. And if the client is very depressed they may not be able to engage in very active therapeutic tasks. In these cases, I should not suggest that the client engages in therapeutic tasks that are too much for them at that point in time. To do so would be to discourage them. I endeavour to monitor my client's frame of mind and encourage them to engage in tasks that are 'challenging but not overwhelming' for them at any given point in time (Dryden, 1985). If I suggest, conversely, that a client engages in insufficiently challenging tasks for them, this may also deprive them of the opportunity of getting the most out of therapy. If a client can easily do something then the therapeutic value of such tasks may be minimal.

5.2 Tasks and therapist expertise

How much of the effectiveness of therapy is dependent on the therapist's expertise? Research shows that the answer is: quite a bit (Beutler et al., 2004). The following is a sample of issues pertaining to therapist expertise in carrying out tasks relevant to the working alliance between my client and myself.

5.2.1 Varying the use of tasks

As clients vary along several dimensions, accordingly I need to vary their own contribution to the therapy process. This has clear implications for client goals as there is more than one way 'to skin a therapeutic cat'. If one set of therapist tasks does not help particular clients then others may. This also has implications for therapeutic bonds. A useful system – called Thinking-Feeling-Action (TFA), which is relevant to the variation of therapist tasks – was devised by Hutchins (1984). Hutchins argued that a therapist can improve the effectiveness of therapy by focusing on tasks that match their client's predominant modes (thinking, feeling or action) unless there is good reason to help them focus on their non-preferred modes. One way that this is manifest with respect to what I do

Goal-directed tasks in therapy   53

is in my use of language – employing cognitively oriented language with a client whose predominant mode is 'T' (thinking), feeling-oriented language with a client whose predominant mode is 'F' (feeling) and action-oriented language with a client whose predominant mode is 'A' (action). From a pluralistic perspective, I explain the rationale for this approach, and seek the client's view on the matter before we make a joint decision concerning mode focus and the choice of tasks we will both carry out.

Although Hutchins focuses on the client's predominant modes of dealing with the world, he points out that therapists also have similar predominant modes. In an ideal world effective therapists would, with equal facility, be able to use cognitive, behavioural and affective tasks, but the fact that therapists have their own limitations means that it is a temptation for them to restrict themselves to using tasks that reflect their predominant orientation (cognitive, emotive or behavioural). Hutchins's (1984) analysis implies that if I restrict myself to using particular intervention modes (i.e. cognitive, emotive or behavioural), I would help a smaller range of clients than if I am more flexible in freely and appropriately using cognitive, emotive and behavioural tasks.

From this it follows that to increase my effectiveness in the task domain of the alliance, I need to acknowledge my own task preferences, while working on broadening my own range of task behaviour. This is a task that itself calls for continual exposure to what a range of therapy models has to offer – a project consistent with the flexible and pluralistic nature of the approach to therapy as outlined in this book. I have come to recognise that I am inclined not to use imagery tasks much in therapy because I do not have a clear and pronounced imagery modality as a person. As a consequence, I remind myself regularly to think about the use of such methods in therapy and discuss their use with my client as a counterpoint to my 'natural' tendency in this area.

My late friend and colleague, Dr Arnold Lazarus (1989) went a step further than Hutchins (1984) by cogently arguing that there are seven modalities of human experience that should be considered when working with clients: Behaviour, Affect (or Emotions), Sensation, Imagery, Cognition (or Thinking), Interpersonal Relationships and Physiological Functioning. These seven modalities are referred to by the acronym BASIC ID (D stands for drugs, the most common way of dealing with problems in the physiological functioning modality). Lazarus argued that people vary according to the modalities they typically use and claimed that it is useful to develop a person's modality profile by asking them to rate themselves on a 0–10 scale indicating varying degree of modality use. I will show you how this informed my work with two

54　Goal-directed tasks in therapy

clients experiencing a similar anger problem. Tony scored highly in the behavioural, interpersonal and sensation modalities. I helped him use these modalities, especially when he first noticed himself getting angry, by encouraging him to use a sensory (in this case, olfactory) cue to relax (his aftershave), before capitalising on his strong tendency to use the behavioural and interpersonal modalities: I encouraged him to use his assertive skills with the person with whom he was angry. This was based on the flexible attitude of 'giving people the right to be wrong', an attitude towards which Tony had much sympathy.

On the other hand, Dennis scored high on the cognitive and imagery modalities, but low on behavioural and interpersonal modalities. I therefore taught Dennis flexible, non-extreme attitudes as a way of dealing with provocations before encouraging him to see himself asserting himself with the person with whom he was angry. Following this I encouraged him to use assertion in real life. Since, in general, people require more help in using tasks in their non-preferred modalities, I spent more time in therapy on teaching Dennis how to assert himself in real life than I did with Tony.

From this it is clear that it is useful for me to know a client's modality strengths in developing a jointly agreed treatment plan. However, I sometimes need to help a client to become more proficient in modalities in which they are less proficient. For instance, a very passive client often needs to learn to be more active in the behavioural modality. Once again, I will put this to the client so that we can discuss it. Indeed, this is particularly important with a passive client because it gives them an opportunity to be more active in the therapy process as a precursor to adopting a more active stance in life.

5.2.2 Therapist styles when working with attitudes and mindsets

A variety of therapist styles that I can use when I am working with a client's attitudes and mindsets have been discussed by DiGiuseppe (1991). The purpose of working with attitudes and mindsets in therapy, as we shall see in Chapters 7 and 8, is to help the client choose which attitude or mindset to be guided by after examining their truth, logical sense and pragmatic value. While it is partly a matter of expertise to know when to use which style, at which part of the therapy process, with which client, I discuss the selection of an appropriate style when working with mindsets and attitudes fully and openly with the client and the decision to employ a particular style with a particular client is made

Goal-directed tasks in therapy 55

with that client. The major styles that I draw upon when working with the client's attitudes and mindsets are as follows.

5.2.2.1 Socratic questioning

Socratic questioning involves my asking questions to guide the client's discovery about the problematic aspects of their rigid, extreme attitudes and the helpful aspects of their flexible, non-extreme attitudes. Beck's Cognitive Therapy and REBT both favour Socratic questioning, but there are times when this questioning style does not result in therapeutic benefit for the client. As DiGiuseppe (1991: 183) notes 'Some clients of limited intelligence, limited creativity or extreme emotional disturbance may not come up with an appropriate answer to a Socratic question.' He adds that letting them suffer because they do not respond well to this interpersonal style of questioning may not be ethical. According to my own way of working, I persist with a particular style for a reasonable amount of time before switching to another style of questioning.

5.2.2.2 Being didactic

In being didactic, I make points declaratively before checking the client's understanding of and response to the point made. I endeavour to make these points simply and briefly, but without being patronising.

5.2.2.3 Being metaphorical

In this case I make a point with reference to a metaphor, story, analogy or parable. This style's main advantage is that it increases the memorability of the point if the method used resonates with the client (Blenkiron, 2010). As before, I need to check the client's understanding and response to the point expressed in the method used. I may otherwise think that the client understands the point being made, when in reality they may not.

5.2.2.4 Using humour

There has been a large amount written on the role of humour in psychotherapy (e.g. Lemma, 1999). Humour can facilitate the working alliance with some clients and can help them to take themselves seriously, though not too seriously and thus encourage them to put their life situation into a healthier perspective (Ellis, 1977). With other clients, however, humour may either increase their tendency to defend themselves against psychological

56 Goal-directed tasks in therapy

pain by the use of minimisation or leave them with the sense that the therapist is ridiculing them. In using humour while working with attitudes and mindsets (and in general), getting client feedback on my use of humour is, therefore, critical.

To DiGiuseppe's list, I would add the following.

5.2.2.5 Using self-disclosure

I am fully prepared to reveal personal information about myself in therapy. I have found this to be a powerful way of encouraging clients to re-evaluate rigid, extreme attitudes and provide one way of dealing with their problems (Dryden, 1990). For instance, I sometimes use a personal example of how I overcame my anxiety about stammering in public. I reveal that I used to believe rigidly that 'I must hide my stammer from others.' I then describe how I questioned this rigid attitude by proving to myself that there was no evidence to support it, that it made no sense and resulted in an increase of anxiety, which only led to me stammering more. I will then go on to say that I changed my attitude: 'There is no reason why I must hide my stammer. If I stammer and people notice, then I won't like it, but so be it.' I then describe how I pushed myself to put this flexible attitude (which was true, sensible and had better pragmatic value for me) into practice in public speaking and I finally outline the productive effects I experienced by so doing.

This is an example of the coping model of therapist self-disclosure where I say, in effect, 'I used to have this problem, but this is what I did to overcome it.' This contrasts with a mastery model of therapist self-disclosure where the therapist reveals that they have never experienced a problem similar to their client's because they have always had a flexible attitude about the issue at hand. The mastery model tends to accentuate the differences between the therapist and their client; in my experience it is less productive than the coping model in encouraging clients to re-evaluate their own rigid, extreme attitudes. Some clients, however, find neither model useful. In that case, I avoid the use of self-disclosure altogether.

5.2.2.6 Being enactive

Actions sometimes speak louder than words in working with a client's attitudes and I may make a point by demonstrating it vividly in action. For instance, if I am struggling to explain the difference between the evaluation of an act and the evaluation of self when helping the client to

distinguish between self-devaluation (an extreme attitude) and unconditional self-acceptance (a non-extreme attitude), I might throw a glass of
water over myself and ask the client whether what I have done is silly.
If they agree that it is, I ask them whether this makes me a silly person
or a fallible human being who can act in silly or non-silly ways. This
can help them see in vivid terms that the latter is the case rather than the
former. It is again helpful for the therapist to gain the client's permission
to demonstrate a point in action before doing so.

5.2.3 Capitalising on the client's learning style and preferred modalities

Therapy tasks (broadly conceptualised), as used here, are the means by
which clients achieve their goals. If clients do so it is because they have
learned something new (for example, to see things differently and/or to
act differently).

When I take a working-alliance perspective on client learning, I consider how best to facilitate learning for each of my clients. For instance,
I need to discover how each of my clients learns and capitalises on this
in the best way by tailoring my interventions accordingly. The best way
to do this, in my view, is to follow George Kelly's advice. Kelly, the
founder of Personal Construct Psychology, argued that 'if you want to
know the answer to a question about a client, then ask them directly,
they just might tell you' (Bannister & Fransella, 1986). I will therefore
begin the discussion on client learning by asking the client how they
learn best and questioning them further about this to bring out the most
important aspects.

I will illustrate this issue by discussing two clients who had similar
problems, but different learning styles. Alan and David both experienced
anxiety about public speaking and therefore avoided it whenever they
could. They were both anxious that they would say something foolish
during formal public speaking. Alan learned best by discovering how
other people had overcome similar fears and then applying from their
experiences what made sense to him. David, meanwhile, said that it
was important to him to discover the possible origins of his fear before
learning how to deal with it. I encouraged Alan to search the Internet to
develop a knowledge base of how others had dealt successfully with this
fear and then to put together a way of dealing with the problem that was
right for him.

I took a very different tack with David by helping him to review
his past experiences of public speaking. He thus discovered that it had

58 Goal-directed tasks in therapy

started when a teacher had commented on his lisp in front of his class-mates, who then started mimicking him. I helped him to understand the rigid, extreme attitudes he had developed as a consequence of this experience and was still unwittingly perpetuating by avoiding public speaking. For David, practising flexible, non-extreme alternatives to these rigid, extreme attitudes while revisiting in imagination that early experience was an important precursor to practising these new attitudes in the present. In contrast, I did not discuss the possible historical roots of Alan's problem because he did not consider this to be an important element in his learning style.

5.2.4 Helping a client to get the most out of their tasks

Assuming a client does have tasks to carry out in FCBT, it is important that I help them derive the most benefit from these tasks. I therefore:

1   endeavour to arrive at a clear shared agreement with the client about their tasks, answering any questions they may have about them;
2   help the client to see the relationship clearly between their tasks and their goals and encourage them to bear this connection carefully in mind during therapy;
3   discover from the client what their strengths and weaknesses are so that together we can modify the client's tasks after taking these into account, but before the client carries out the tasks;
4   work with the client to modify a task based on the client's feedback on their experience of carrying it out;
5   train the client in their tasks if they are relevant (Dryden (2004) provides an example of training clients to become proficient in client tasks);
6   problem-solve any obstacles with the client to task execution, both in advance and when they occur;
7   have alternative client tasks in mind if the client is unable to carry out their original tasks;
8   ensure that during homework task negotiation with the client they can specify what they are going to do, when they are going to do it and how often.

5.2.5 Using tasks at different stages of change

I have to bear in mind the fact that not only my tasks as a therapist but also my client's tasks may change during therapy.

Goal-directed tasks in therapy   59

5.2.5.1 My tasks in therapy

I begin by considering my tasks as therapist. I have organised these according to the stage of therapy in which such tasks are most salient. Please remember that this does not mean that I don't use such tasks in the other phases (see Table 5.1).

5.2.5.2 The client's tasks in FCBT

Table 5.2 lists the tasks that clients have agreed to carry out in therapy.

The tasks at the top reflect those that are more salient at the beginning. Further down the list are those tasks that are more relevant later in the process. Once again, please remember that this does not mean that tasks

Table 5.1 My tasks as a therapist across the therapeutic process

The beginning stage

- Establish a therapeutic alliance
- Outline the pluralistic and flexible nature of how I work and the implications for myself and my client
- Begin to assess and intervene on target problem
- Teach the ABCs models of disturbance and health
- Negotiate homework tasks appropriate to the beginning phase
- Identify and deal with obstacles to change

The middle stage

- Follow through on target problem
- Encourage the client to engage in relevant tasks that are selected jointly by both of us
- Work on client's other problems
- Identify and examine specific and, where relevant, core rigid and extreme attitudes
- Negotiate homework tasks appropriate to the middle stage
- Identify and deal with obstacles to change
- Encourage the client to maintain and enhance gains
- Undertake relapse prevention and deal with vulnerability factors
- Encourage the client to become their own therapist

The ending stage

- Decide with the client on when and how to end
- Encourage the client to summarise what has been learned
- Attribute improvement to client's efforts
- Deal with obstacles to ending
- Agree on criteria for follow-ups and for resuming therapy

60 Goal-directed tasks in therapy

Table 5.2 The client's tasks across the therapeutic process

Specify problems
Be open to the ABC framework
Provide their own views about salient aspects of the therapeutic process
Apply the specific principle of emotional responsibility
Apply the principle of therapeutic responsibility
Disclose doubts, difficulties and blocks to change
Identify and deal with obstacles to change
Generalise learning
Undertake relapse prevention and deal with vulnerability factors
Take responsibility for becoming their own therapist
Seek therapy in the future when self-help fails

listed at the top are not salient later on in the process, and vice versa to some degree. In Chapter 9 I will discuss these tasks in greater detail.

I will consider the role in Chapter 6 that context plays in people's problems and how I tend to work with context in therapy.

Chapter 6

The importance of context in FCBT

I once saw a poster that left a lasting impression on me. It showed a uniformed white policeman running behind a black man who was dressed in casual clothes. The inference to be drawn from this was that the white policeman was chasing the black man. But around the corner there was another poster in which the white policeman and the casually dressed black man were running behind a casually dressed white man. It transpired, when the captions were revealed, that the casually dressed black man was a plain clothed policeman and that he and the uniformed policeman were chasing the casually dressed white man. This poster illustrated powerfully the importance of context in understanding phenomena and how easy it is to make inferences based on only a part of the context: such inferences may radically change when the full context is revealed. In this chapter I will consider the importance of working with context in the way I work. The chief points I want to make here are that: (1) there are different ways of working with context rather than one correct way and (2) my client and I need to discuss context and then agree on ways of dealing with it during therapy. The way of dealing with it may change from situation to situation.

6.1 The context of clients' problems can be specific or general

Clients who discuss their problems with me normally locate this discussion within a context. Such a context can either be specific or general. Because, however, most clients tend to discuss their problems in broad terms, the context may well be general. If I want to learn more about my client's problem and the specific dynamics involved, I will need to encourage the client to come up with a specific example of the problem under discussion. By this I mean an example of how the problem is

62 The importance of context in FCBT

experienced by the client in a specific situation with a specific person or persons (if relevant) involved. A good method of bringing this to mind is to use the game known as Cluedo[1] in which a murder has been committed. The purpose of the game is to guess the murderer's identity, the room in which the murder occurred and the murder weapon used (e.g. It was Professor Plum in the conservatory with a revolver). I endeavour to establish this level of specificity when it is needed, as it will stand me in good stead in helping my clients get the most out of therapy.

When a client discusses their problems in general terms, in contrast, although the type of situations in which the person experiences their general problems is usually clear, the context described lacks a specific referent. For example, Susan came to therapy for help with her public-speaking anxiety. When I encouraged her to discuss this problem she told me that she became anxious whenever she had to give a presentation when she knew her bosses would be present. Even though the type of situation is clear, the general nature of this described problem should be noted. When I asked her to discuss a concrete example of the problem, Susan chose the most recent example, which had happened the day before in the boardroom when her 'big boss' (as she called him) was present. Here, Susan was able to identify a specific situation (giving a presentation in the boardroom the day before) and the presence of a specific person featuring in her anxiety description (i.e. her big boss).

You may find it useful to note that when clients are asked to discuss concrete examples of their target problem, they tend to drift back to discussing these problems in general terms and in general contexts. I bear this tendency in mind and therefore encourage clients to give me permission to help them to remain focused on the specifics of their target problem.

I have particular views concerning when it is best to work with specific contexts and when to work with general contexts, but I am nevertheless willing to make compromises with these views if a client is unwilling to go along with these ideas. The pluralistic nature of this work is present when I provide the client with a rationale for the level of work we have suggested between us and I also fully engage the client in a discussion if there is disagreement between us. I adopt an experimental attitude with my client and, if necessary, agree to go along with the client's preferences and see what happens when doing so. Taking this stance serves to maintain the working alliance between us, as was discussed in Chapters 2–5.

I prefer to work within a specific context of my client's problems when I consider it is important to engage the client's feelings in the process of therapy. This is usually the case when I first begin to work

The importance of context in FCBT   63

with a client's problem. By dealing with a specific context in which the client experienced their problem, both the client and I are able to identify and work with specific feelings, thought and behaviours. The more specific the information the client provides, the more likely it is that I will be able to encourage the client to begin to think, feel and act differently.

In contrast to this, I prefer to work with general contexts when encouraging my client to *generalise* their learning from one particular context to other, similar contexts. However, as I have said previously, even though I may have good reason to work with a specific or general context at a particular point in time and may provide the client with a rationale for doing so, the client may prefer to do just the opposite. As I have discussed in Chapters 2–5, I take into account the working alliance between my client and myself throughout therapy and while I may suggest a particular strategy, I will not press the point if doing so threatens the working alliance between us.

I will now provide an example of how I made flexible use of the context of a client's problem in therapy. I introduced Susan earlier in Chapter 2 and have mentioned her again in this chapter. She came to therapy for help with public speaking anxiety and I began by asking her to discuss a specific example of her problem. She responded by discussing a recent example where she had become anxious about speaking in front of a group where her 'big boss' was present. After discussing this specific example with Susan, I enquired to what extent this situation was typical of her public-speaking anxiety. It transpired that the important element of situations where Susan became anxious about speaking in public was the presence of a superior who Susan considered might affect her future career. I used this information here to encourage Susan to speak at events where her bosses were present, so that she could be armed with new ways of dealing with such a situation. I proceeded in this way because it made sense to Susan. Had that not been the case, I might have started, with her agreement, by assessing general contexts in which Susan became anxious about speaking in public and I would have used this general information to plan more specific interventions.

6.2 Contexts: descriptions or inferences

When a client describes a context in which they are experiencing a problem, irrespective of whether the context described is general or specific, I bear in mind the fact that although this context seems very real to the client, their description of what happened may well be an inference and may therefore be inaccurate.

6.2.1 Descriptions of contexts

In *describing* a context in which their problem occurred, a client is referring to aspects that could theoretically be verified by a video camera with an audio channel. This was called the 'camera check' by Maxie C. Maultsby (1975). In such cases the client may be accurate or inaccurate in their description. Thus, if Susan was describing a context in which she experienced public-speaking anxiety, she might say: 'I got anxious just before giving a speech in the boardroom where four of my bosses were present.' This constitutes a description because it can be factually verified. If it is correct, then we can say that Susan gave an accurate account of the context. On the other hand, if it was incorrect (e.g. three of her bosses were present not four) then we can say that Susan gave an inaccurate description of the context. However, irrespective of whether it was accurate or inaccurate, Susan's statement was a description of the context because she did not go beyond the data at hand.

6.2.2 Inferences about contexts

When I ask a client to describe a specific context of their problem, they may well go beyond the data at hand and make an inference regarding the context. In contrast to a description, an *inference* is a hunch about the context that goes beyond what can be described accurately. This inference may be accurate or inaccurate and as such needs to be checked against available data. However, given that it is an interpretation, an inference can rarely be factually verified but can be accepted as probably true (if the data seem to confirm it) or as probably false (if the data seem to disconfirm it).

I will now show you what I mean. Let's suppose that when I asked Susan to describe a specific context of her public-speaking anxiety, she said: 'I got anxious about giving my talk when I saw that my bosses were in the audience and thought they would be critical of my presentation.' If we subject this statement to the 'camera-audio check', we can say that Susan did describe the presence of her bosses in the audience, but if we examine part of this statement closely – 'and thought that they would be critical of my presentation' – we can see that this does not pass this check. This is because this statement is really an inference about her bosses' reaction towards her and it goes beyond the data at hand. It therefore needs to be regarded as a hypothesis about reality rather than a descriptive statement of reality. As I mentioned earlier, such a hypothesis needs to be tested against the available data. Thus, Susan needs to ask herself what evidence she has that her bosses would be critical of her performance. The data she puts forward need to be considered carefully regarding whether it confirms or disconfirms the hypothesis. Once all the data are in and have been analysed, Susan can then come up with what has been called the 'best bet', i.e. the conclusion that best fits the data. In order for Susan to do this, she needs to be in an objective frame of mind, which may be difficult for her to achieve, because when she is relating the incident under consideration she may well be in a subjective, disturbed state of mind.

6.3 Two major ways of dealing with inferences about contexts

It goes without saying that in individual therapy, the client is the only person who is describing the contexts in which they experience their problems. There is therefore no actual independent authority to whom we can refer regarding the accuracy or otherwise of the inferences the client makes. What is important is that when the client expresses an inference about reality rather than a description of reality, I am clear in my own mind that this is an inference and that it may therefore be accurate or inaccurate. If I agree – wrongly – with the client that their inference is a fact without further examination, then, in my view, this compromises the therapeutic work that I need to do with the client.

It will sometimes be clear to me that what I have called the 'colouring process' is at work and the client's disturbance (based as it is on rigidity) 'colours' the inferences that they make about reality and I will discuss this point later in this chapter. However, it is often not so clear and I therefore need to explore this issue further with the client. The question of when this exploration is to be done is an interesting point as it raises the issue of how I can respond best to a client's inferences about the contexts of their problems. This will be the subject of the next section. Once I have helped my client to understand that the inferences that they typically make in problem situations are coloured by rigidity, how can I help the client to deal with these inferences? We have already seen two ways of doing so. First, encourage them to assume temporarily that their inference is true and then to identify and respond to the rigid attitudes that they hold towards the inference. Second, have them examine the inference itself against the available evidence. While in practice I prefer the former approach, since doing so helps both my client and myself to deal with the client's disturbed reaction to the 'assumed to be true' inference, in pluralistic practice I will involve the client in a discussion of the best order for the client.

66 The importance of context in FCBT

6.3.1 Assume temporarily that the client's inference is correct

As a way of responding to a client's inference about the context of one of her problems I may assume temporarily that their inference is correct. Practitioners of Rational Emotive Behaviour Therapy (REBT) do this as a matter of course, because their initial therapeutic interest is to help the client identify the irrational beliefs that are considered to form the basis of the client's emotional problem. When my goal therefore is to help the client discover the rigidity at the core of their problem I will take a leaf out of the REB therapist's book and encourage myself and my client to do the same: to assume temporarily that the client's inference is correct. At this point if I encourage the client to examine this inference I will then impede the process of identifying the client's rigid attitude. Although I am pursuing the identical strategy here, I am more likely to engage the client in a discussion of this strategy and therefore more likely to involve the client in a joint agreement to implement the strategy than my REBT colleagues.

I will now show how I implemented this principle in dealing with Susan's stated inference. The following dialogue occurred after Susan and I had discussed the two ways of dealing with her inference and agreed to implement the 'let's assume that your inference was correct' strategy.

Windy: So, Susan, you have said that you became anxious when you saw your bosses in attendance and thought that they would be critical of your performance. Is that right?

Susan: Yes, that's right.

Windy: I expect you had no way of knowing that for certain, but let's assume temporarily that you were correct and that they would be critical of your performance. We can discuss what led you to think that later, but for now, let's assume that you were right. OK?

Susan: OK.

Sometimes a client may react adversely to this 'let's assume temporarily that you were right' approach to their context-related inference should they think I disbelieve them. This is more likely to happen if I have not provided a rationale and discussed it with the client, but chosen instead to proceed unilaterally. This negative reaction, however, can still happen when agreement based on negotiation has taken place. If this occurs, it is important for me to explain that I am not adopting a disbelieving stance and that the reason I am taking this approach is to help both the client and myself determine whether the client is being flexible or rigid about

The importance of context in FCBT   67

this inference. Bear in mind that a core assumption of my work is that rigidity is at the root of emotional disturbance. It is therefore possible for Susan to infer that her bosses would be critical of her performance, but for her to take a flexible attitude towards this inference and therefore not be unhealthily anxious about this prospect.

On other occasions, this 'let's assume' approach may lead directly to the client expressing the view that their inference causes their emotional disturbance. This provides with me with an opportunity to (1) educate the client about the core assumption of how I work concerning what largely determines emotional disturbance and (2) assess which attitude Susan was adopting in the context being discussed. For example:

Windy: So, let's assume temporarily that your bosses would be critical of your performance.

Susan: That would mean that I would have to be anxious.

Windy: How?

Susan: Well their criticism would make me anxious.

[*Here Susan is advancing an 'inference causes disturbance' model.*]

Windy: Well, that is one model to explain your anxiety. This model states, as you say, that the reason you are anxious is that you infer that a threat is on the horizon, in your case the criticism that you thought you would get from your bosses. But there is another model I would like to discuss with you if you were interested?

[Note that I ask Susan for permission to proceed.]

Susan: Sure.

Windy: OK. This model states that in anxiety the presence of a threat is an important ingredient of your anxiety, but it isn't sufficient to explain it. Should we take this approach, we would argue that it is the attitude you take towards the threat that is the central ingredient. Shall I go on?

Susan: Yes, please do.

Windy: OK, in Flexibility-Based CBT, we say that there are three possible attitudes you can take towards a threat, in your case being criticised by your bosses. One may be implausible but I will discuss it anyway and the other two are more plausible candidates. The implausible attitude is indifference. In that case you do not care if your bosses are critical of your performance or not.

68   The importance of context in FCBT

Susan: That's ridiculous.

Windy: I agree, because in your case it would involve your lying to yourself and trying to convince yourself that you don't care whether or not your bosses are critical of your performance when you obviously do care.

Susan: Agreed.

Windy: So that leaves the two plausible options. The first is the rigid attitude. Here your attitude is that it is absolutely crucial for your bosses not to be critical of your presentation. You recognise that it is possible for them to criticise you. But at the same time you are trying to eliminate it either in reality, as a possibility in your mind or by avoiding it. In the short term this attitude may keep you safe, but in the long term it does not work. In fact, the rigid attitude will lead you to keep thinking of your bosses' criticism, to overestimate its occurrence and to exaggerate the extent of such criticism. Adopting this attitude means that you do not get much practice at dealing with such criticism in a constructive manner, since you are always trying to avoid it. But in doing so, you only practise disturbing yourself about it.

Susan: That certainly seems to describe my approach to criticism from my bosses. What's the other plausible option?

Windy: That's the flexible attitude. In this case you acknowledge that you don't like to be criticised, but you don't go out of your way to eliminate it either in reality, from your mind or by avoidant behaviour. You acknowledge that this criticism may occur, but because you are flexible in your attitude towards it you are also more objective about the chances of it happening and about the extent of it, should it happen. Adopting this attitude means that you get more practice at dealing with such criticism in a constructive manner, since you are more likely to face up to it.

Susan: Well, that attitude seems to be the best one of the three on offer, although I wish I was so good at presentations that I could guarantee that I wouldn't be criticised.

Windy: If I could give you that I would be a magician rather than a therapist. But seriously, which of the three attitudes I have outlined will help you improve your presentation skills?

Susan: The flexible attitude.

Windy: Why?

Susan: Because it's the only one that is realistic and which will lead me to do presentations so that I can gain experience at doing them and learn from my experiences and from the feedback given to me by others.

6.3.2 Examine the inference

Another way of dealing with a client's inference about a context, especially when it appears to be distorted, is for me to help them to stand back and review the inference with respect to the available evidence to judge its probable accuracy or inaccuracy.

I agree with those of my REBT colleagues who argue that the best time for clients to examine their inferences is when they have adopted a flexible attitude towards the inference as opposed to a rigid attitude. However, I also think that, although the constructs of therapists are important to consider, such constructs should be thought about alongside working alliance considerations (see, in particular, Chapter 3). Clients' views thus need to be taken seriously in therapy and a negotiation between my client and myself is needed when we disagree over a way forward. If a mutually satisfactory solution cannot be found, I will act to preserve the alliance.

The following is an example of how to deal with a client's inference about the context in which their problem occurred.

Windy: So, Susan, you said that you were anxious about giving a presentation where you thought that your bosses who were in attendance would criticise you. Is that right?

Susan: Yes, that's correct.

Windy: If you stand back for a moment do you think that it was a fact that they would criticise your performance or do you think it was your hunch about the situation?

Susan: Probably a hunch, but a correct one.

Windy: Well, shall we look together at the evidence for and against your hunch?

Susan: OK, fair enough.

Windy: What is the evidence in favour of your hunch that your bosses would criticise your presentation?

Susan: Well, I would criticise it if I were in their shoes.

Windy: What other evidence do you have?

Susan: Just a gut feeling that they would.

Windy: OK. And what evidence do you have that they wouldn't criticise your performance?

Susan: Well, I haven't heard them criticise anybody else's presentation.

Windy: And as bosses go, are they particularly critical, encouraging or neutral?

Susan: Well, my 'big boss' is pretty encouraging, one of the others is too, and the third is more neutral.

70 The importance of context in FCBT

Windy: So, none of them are particularly critical?
Susan: No.
Windy: Any other evidence for or against?
Susan: No.
Windy: So, let's review the evidence for and against. In favour of the idea that your bosses would criticise your presentation is the idea that you yourself would be critical of your performance if you were in their shoes and also your gut feeling that you have that they would be critical. Against your hunch is the fact that you have not heard them be critical of anyone else's presentation and that as bosses go two are pretty encouraging and one is neutral. So, what would you conclude from this evidence?
Susan: That my hunch is probably wrong.

Let me repeat that if the client is to evaluate such evidence objectively then they need to be in an objective, non-disturbed frame of mind to do so. For that reason it is better for me to first help the client to adopt a flexible attitude towards the inference rather than a rigid one. However, as I mention throughout the book, FCBT's preferred strategy should not override more pluralistic concerns such as the client's view of how best to proceed.

6.4 When inferences are coloured by rigidity

When a client reports a problem and describes its context, I have argued that they may well tell me about their *inference* concerning what happened rather than a *description* of what happened. But how can we explain why the client makes such an inference in the first place, particularly when it appears to be distorted? One reason is that such inferences are often coloured by the client's rigid thinking when the client faces an ambiguous situation. As discussed in Chapter 1, in the way I work, rigidity is at the heart of psychological disturbance and leads a person to be polarised in their thinking.

Let me exemplify this process with Susan. When she said that she got anxious because she saw that her bosses were in the audience and that they would be critical of her, she thought she was describing reality. In fact, as we have seen, Susan was making an inference about their response to her which may or may not have been accurate. This is how we can explain why Susan made such an inference.

Susan held a rigid attitude towards being criticised and also believed that being criticised defined her self-worth. The attendance of her bosses at her presentation proved ambiguous for her. Her bosses therefore might

The importance of context in FCBT   71

criticise her or they might not. However, because Susan could not convince herself that her bosses would not criticise her, her rigid attitude towards being criticised led her to infer that they would criticise her and she treated this as a fact.

This is how this principle works step by step:

1 Susan is disturbed about being criticised.
2 She is therefore rigid about being criticised.
3 This rigidity about being criticised is latent and will be activated when there is a possibility that Susan will be criticised.
4 In giving a talk in front of her bosses she is faced with an ambiguous situation.
5 Because Susan is rigid about being criticised and cannot convince herself that her bosses will not criticise her, her polarised thinking (which stems from her rigidity) leads her to assume that they will criticise her and that this is a fact. Note that it does not occur to Susan that she can be in an ambiguous situation with respect to being criticised and still not be criticised. She will be much more able to entertain this possibility as she develops a flexible approach to being criticised.

I call this a 'colouring' process and it is particularly evident when a client makes the same inferences across situations. In such cases, the client holds a rigid attitude that is more general in nature. It therefore transpired that Susan frequently made inferences that people would criticise her. This tendency to make such inferences in ambiguous situations stemmed from her general rigid attitude that she must not be criticised by people whose opinion of her she cared about.

6.4.1 Educating clients about this colouring process

I have already discussed two ways in this chapter to help clients deal with their inferences: (1) to assume that they are true to enable them to identify their rigid attitudes that they hold about these inferences and (2) to examine them when they appear to be distorted. In this section, I will discuss a third way, which involves helping clients understand why they make the same inferences time and again. For this I need to do the following:

1 Help the client see that the specific inferences they keep making represent a more general theme (for instance, failure, rejection or, in Susan's case, criticism).

72 The importance of context in FCBT

2   Show the client that they hold two general rigid attitudes: one towards the theme itself (for instance, 'I must not be rejected') and the other towards certainty and the lack of it, related to the theme (for instance, 'I must know that I won't be rejected').

3   Show the client that they bring these two general rigid attitudes to specific situations in which the possibility exists that the event embodied in the theme may occur (for instance, that it is possible that she may be rejected).

4   Then help them to understand that because they cannot convince themselves that the event embodied in the theme won't happen, they think that it will (for instance, that she predicts that she will be rejected because she cannot convince herself that she won't be).

5   Show them that they have unwittingly taught themselves to see uncertainty as a portent of adversity (for instance, if I am uncertain that I will be rejected, then I will be rejected).

6.4.2 Dealing with inferences that are coloured by rigidity

Once I have helped my client to understand that the inferences they typically make in problem situations are coloured by rigidity, how can I help the client to deal with these inferences? We have already seen two ways of doing so. First, encourage them to assume temporarily that their inference is true and then to identify and respond to the rigid attitudes they hold towards the inference. This is particularly recommended when helping the client to deal with specific examples of their problem. Earlier in this chapter I showed how to do this with Susan. Second, help them to examine the inference. Again, this is carried out most effectively when dealing with specific examples of her problem as such examination is best done when there are specific data to consider.

The third way of dealing with inferences coloured by rigidity is best done when it is apparent that the client typically makes very similar inferences across problem situations. In Susan's case, she tends to infer criticism when she is in situations where her performance may be evaluated by people whose opinion she cares about. In this situation, after educating the client how this colouring process works (see above), I proceed as follows.

1   I help the client to identify the theme of the inferences they tend to make (for instance, criticism, in the case of Susan).

2   I help them see that they hold rigid attitudes towards both the theme and uncertainty in relation to the theme (e.g. in Susan's case: 'I must not be criticised' and 'I must know that I will not be criticised').

3 I help them to see the impact of these beliefs on the inferences that they tend to make in problem-related situations.
4 I help the client to develop flexible alternatives to these rigid attitudes (in Susan's case, 'I would prefer not to be criticised, but this doesn't mean that I must not be' and 'I would like to know that I won't be criticised, but I don't need to know this').
5 I help the client to see that holding these flexible attitudes allows her to entertain the inference that the adversity that she predicts will happen may not happen (e.g. in Susan's case that she may not be criticised, unless there is good evidence that she will be).
6 I ask the client to choose which attitudes she would like to develop and which she would like to move away from.
7 I help the client to develop the flexible attitudes if she has nominated those (see Chapter 7 for a detailed discussion on how to help clients address their rigid attitudes).
8 If the client has nominated the rigid attitudes, I need to understand and help the client to understand the reasons why and proceed accordingly (see Chapter 8 for a discussion on this point).

6.5 Dealing with inferences that are highly distorted and skewed to the negative

I have considered so far how to deal with inferences when they occur at 'A' in the ABC model that I use in my work. However, they can also occur at 'C' in the model and when they do in an episode of psychological disturbance, they are often highly distorted and skewed to the negative because they are the outcome of processing of 'A' by rigid, extreme attitudes at 'B'.

6.5.1 An example of highly distorted inferences at 'C' and the dangers of treating them as an 'A'

As discussed in the Appendix, cognitions can be found at 'C' in the ABC model of psychological disturbance and health that I use in my work. In an episode of psychological disturbance, while inferences at 'A' may well be distorted, inferences at 'C' are likely to be highly distorted and skewed to the negative. I can generally make this distinction for myself and help my client to make it, while a less experienced novice therapist may put these highly distorted cognitive 'C's at 'A', encourage their client to assume that they are true and thus run into great difficulty clinically.

74 The importance of context in FCBT

For example, let's suppose that a client reports that she (in this case) was panicking the night before. Not unreasonably, the novice therapist asks the client what she was panicking about, to which the client responds that she was most scared of dying from a heart attack. This is an inference, of course, so by using the 'let's assume your inference is true' strategy the novice therapist encourages the client to assume temporarily that she will die from a heart attack as a way of identifying her rigid, extreme attitudes about what the therapist thinks is an 'A'. Indeed, from one perspective it is an 'A', but it is most probably a highly distorted cognitive consequence (at 'C') of a prior rigid, extreme attitude about a less distorted 'A'. It is this standpoint that is more likely to yield the best results clinically in this given situation. The therapist is otherwise faced with the situation of helping the client to take a flexible position towards dying from a heart attack – which is possible, but unlikely. This example shows that highly distorted inferences are often best conceptualised as cognitive consequences (i.e. 'C') of rigid, extreme attitudes towards less distorted inferences at 'A' and dealt with accordingly.

6.5.2 Dealing with highly distorted cognitive 'C's

With highly distorted cognitive consequences of rigid, extreme attitudes at 'C', at first I would teach a client to understand why these thoughts are so distorted (i.e. they are the product of rigid, extreme attitudes). I would then help them to use the presence of these thoughts to identify the rigid, extreme attitudes that have spawned them and then to employ a change-based focus (CBF)[2] with these attitudes (see Chapter 7). I may then help them to use the same change-based focus to respond to these cognitive 'C's, but to recognise that these thoughts may still reverberate in their mind. At that point I would encourage them to switch to an acceptance-based focus (ABF). This reverberation is a natural process, as the mind does not switch off from such thoughts just because CBF methods have been successfully used on any one occasion.

In this chapter, so far, I have discussed four ways that I deal with inferences in how I work: (1) assuming that they are accurate and using them to identify relevant specific rigid attitudes; (2) examining them; (3) if they recur at 'A', showing how they are coloured by general rigid attitudes and how they can be framed more realistically by developing flexible alternatives to these attitudes; and (4) when they are highly distorted, they should be regarded as cognitive consequences (at 'C') of rigid, extreme attitudes and dealt with in a number of ways.

The importance of context in FCBT   75

While I have my own criteria for when to deal with inferences and in which way, as I am flexible and pluralistic I will explain these criteria to the client as explicitly and as free from jargon as I can, and will involve the client throughout in a discussion concerning how best to view inferences in therapy and how best to deal with them. Theoretically, my view is that when a client is emotionally disturbed, inferences are the royal road to the identification of rigid, extreme attitudes that are at the core of such disturbance. In Chapters 7 and 8, I will focus on how I work with these attitudes in therapy. However, I first need to discuss the process whereby clients may create contexts by the way they act in the world and, in particular, towards other people.

6.6 The client's behaviour can help bring about contexts

It is likely that when a client seeks help from me they are disturbed (at 'C' in the ABC framework) about an actual or inferred adversity at 'A' due largely to them holding a set of rigid, extreme attitudes towards the adversity. The focus here is on how the client responds to 'A'. However, it is important to consider the role the client has in creating the 'A' to which they then respond. I mean by this that it is no accident that clients repeatedly find themselves in contexts where the same adversities occur. Rather than being 'bad luck', this is a process that can be understood by examining the client's behaviour, not as a behavioural consequence at 'C', but as ways in which the client, often unintentionally, brings about contexts in which adversities tend to recur.

6.6.1 'I keep being hurt'

Some clients in therapy report a history of being hurt by people. Is this just bad luck or is something more tangible going on here? I will provide an example. Tina came to see me saying that every time she begins a relationship she is hopeful, gives everything to the guy, but ends up getting hurt. As she recounted her history of relationships the following pattern emerged, which revealed that she was not unlucky, but unwittingly helped to bring about the very contexts about which she was disturbed.

When Tina met a new man, he generally treated her well and with respect and she was happy to begin a relationship with him. Then, when they were in a relationship, the man would begin to take her for granted ('A1').[3] Tina would initially respond to this by doing nothing ('C1'),

76 The importance of context in FCBT

hoping that by ignoring the man's behaviour, it would go away. However, it didn't go away; rather, he then began to neglect Tina by phoning her less and making less of an effort to see her ('A2'). Tina responded to this neglect by chasing the man, hoping to show him that she really cared about him ('C2'). This only resulted in the man mistreating Tina even more. He would make dates with her and break them at the last minute or he would call her late at night wanting to see her for sex ('A3'). As she was only too pleased to hear from him, Tina would agree to see him and invariably have sex with him ('C3'). At this point, the only contact the man would initiate with her was these late-night 'booty-calls'; otherwise he would ignore her ('A4'). Tina responded to his lack of contact by increasing her contact with him. She would frequently text him and call him, leaving imploring messages on his answer phone asking him to call her ('C4'). At this point, Tina would discover that he had been seeing another woman ('A5') and would respond with feelings of hurt, thinking that she had been mistreated once more, which proved that nobody would ever want her ('C5'). When she came to therapy, she reported only 'A5'–'C5' and it was only when the therapist wanted to understand this episode in a wider context that the whole picture emerged and that Tina, by her responses at 'C' had unwittingly contributed to the contexts where a man increasingly treated her badly. So, far from being unlucky or a passive victim, Tina was an active contributor to her problem. Although it does not seem to be the case, this is actually good news for Tina. That is because, if she actively even though unintentionally contributes to her problem ('being let down and mistreated by men'), she can change the way she acts and thus deal with the problem more effectively.

What I did to help Tina was (1) to invite her to identify more functional behavioural responses to each of the 'A's listed above and then (2) to work with her to discover the inferences she would make and the attitudes she would hold that would prevent her from making those functional responses. Thus, I not only help clients deal with their dysfunctional responses to adversities, but I also help them deal with the obstacles to functional responding that would help to prevent the adversities.

6.6.2 Interpersonal stance and pull

There is another related area where a client may unwittingly bring about contexts about which they have problems. This concerns what may be seen as the client's 'interpersonal stance'. The client acts towards others in a way that tends to 'pull' a response from others and this response may provide a problematic context for person. So when a client talks about having no friends, I need to discover what the client's interpersonal stance is that might 'pull' a moving away response from other people. For instance, such a person may be unfriendly towards others or may fail to give them suitable 'approach' signals. When the client's relevant interpersonal stance has been identified, along with a more functional alternative stance, the client and I can then investigate the relevant inferences and attitudes that could underlie the problematic stance and those that could underlie the more functional alternative. We may from there investigate both sets of inferences and attitudes as a prelude to changing the problematic interpersonal stance (Kiesler, 1996).

6.6.3 The 'need' for familiarity

The final way that a client may end up by contributing to problematic contexts is explained by the 'need for familiarity'. Here, the argument goes, we seek out contexts that are familiar to us because (1) we implicitly value the familiar even though it may be problematic for us; (2) we are able to predict the world, which is comforting to us even though the context is problematic; (3) we have a well-known 'script' for the way we think, feel and behave and again this is comforting, though problematic. Freud called this phenomenon 'repetition compulsion' and it does seem to provide the answer to the question regarding why some clients keep on making the same mistake over and over again. Here, I will use this concept to see if it makes sense to the client and help the person tolerate the 'unfamiliar' while working to change.

In Chapter 7, I will discuss how I help my clients deal with their problematic attitudes. These, in my view, constitute the core of my therapeutic work.

Chapter 7

Working with rigid and flexible attitudes and mindsets in therapy

As discussed in the Appendix, the ABC model of psychological disturbance and health is based on the saying attributed to Epictetus: 'People are disturbed not by things, but by their views of things.' While this saying indicates 'views' as the core of disturbance – or what I refer to as 'attitudes' in the way that I work – it does not reflect the active role of the person in the disturbance-creating process. I would argue that people disturb themselves about adversities and do so because of the rigid, extreme attitudes they hold towards these adversities. I would further argue that people can un-disturb themselves about the same adversities and can do so by developing an alternative set of flexible, non-extreme attitudes.

In this chapter I will show how I work with rigid attitudes with the expressed purpose of helping clients to develop greater attitudinal flexibility. In Chapter 8, I will focus on how I work with clients' extreme attitudes with the purpose of helping them develop healthy, realistic and sensible non-extreme attitudes. All this work is predicated on the premise that clients understand the role such attitudes play in their problems and their potential solutions and have modified the form and content of these attitudes in the assessment process with me to reflect their specific problems.

I will also show, in addition to discussing how I work with rigid attitudes, how I work with related fixed 'mindsets'. This is a broader term than 'attitudes' and encompasses such concepts as 'outlook' and 'perspective'.

7.1 The emphasis of choice in the attitudes taken towards adversities

In arguing that human beings have a choice concerning the attitudes that we take towards the adversities that we encounter, I take an existential position. This has been eloquently expressed by Victor Frankl, who famously wrote: 'Everything can be taken from a man but one thing: the

Working with rigid and flexible attitudes   79

last of the human freedoms – to choose one's attitude in any given set of circumstances, to choose one's own way' (Frankl, 1984).

I will discuss this issue of attitude choice more carefully as it is an important concept to understand if I am to encourage a client to take a *realistic* approach to attitude change in therapy. In doing so, I will concentrate on how I work with rigid and flexible attitudes and mindsets in this chapter. In Chapter 8 I will discuss how I work with the major forms of extreme and non-extreme attitudes that seem to be derived from the rigid and flexible attitudes lying at the core of psychological disturbance and health respectively.

7.2 The emphasis of choice in the rigid and flexible attitudes taken towards adversities

In discussing the issue of choice with the client, it is important that I help the client to see that the first choice they have when being helped to deal with their target problem is between the rigid attitude that underpins their problem and the alternative flexible attitude that underpins the potential solution to this problem.

7.2.1 Helping the client to see the difference between attitudinal flexibility and attitudinal rigidity (the two options)

During the first stage in working with a client's rigid and flexible attitudes I help them see clearly the difference between attitudinal rigidity and attitudinal flexibility, which are the only two options available given the person's preference. Choosing between such attitudes is facilitated when the client really understands the differences between the two options.

In doing this, I will help the client to understand that both attitudes are based on a sense of what is important to them or to their preference. A client thus has preferences for certain conditions to exist in life and for other conditions not to exist. These preferences range from being mild to very strong in intensity according to the relationship of the conditions to the person's personal domain.[1]

7.2.2 Preferences: not a target for change in FCBT

When a person seeks help for a specific problem, I assume that something is important to that person, something that they want. This is the case whether the person is disturbed about the adversity involved in the problem or whether they respond to the adversity constructively. Let's

80 Working with rigid and flexible attitudes

take the example of Susan, whom we have already met in the book.[2] If you recall, Susan came to therapy for help with her public-speaking anxiety. In the specific episode that she and I chose to focus on, Susan was anxious about her performance being criticised by her bosses who would be at her presentation. So, what do we know? We know it is important to Susan that her bosses are not critical of her. This is what she prefers not to happen to her, but she is not indifferent to this. If she was, she would not care whether they were critical of her performance or not.

Can we say that people can choose to change what is important to them or their preferences? Does it make sense, for example, to say that Susan can choose to find the absence of criticism from her bosses unimportant, when we know that it is important to her? In my view, this clearly does not make much sense. How can Susan find absence of criticism from her bosses unimportant? How can she persuade herself not to care about something that she cares about? At a personal level, I don't know and this is not the issue. I accept a client's preference and what they find important and do not see this as a target for change. If I do not encourage the client to change their preferences, then the object of change lies elsewhere. It lies with the two ways in which people deal with their preferences

7.2.3 The choice: keeping preferences flexible vs making preferences rigid

A preference or sense of importance is common, then, to both psychological disturbance and psychological health. What distinguishes between health and disturbance is whether a person can retain what is important to them (i.e. their preference) and keep this flexible rather than make it rigid. In Susan's case, her disturbance-promoting rigid attitude begins with a statement of what is important to her and of what she wants: 'It is important to me that my bosses do not criticise my performance and I don't want this to happen . . .' and then ends with a statement that makes it clear that she has made her preference rigid: '. . . and therefore they must not do so'. Compare this with what could be Susan's health-promoting flexible attitude. Note that this too begins with the same statement of importance: 'It is important to me that my bosses do not criticise my performance and I don't want this to happen . . .' and then ends with a statement that makes it clear that she has kept her preference rigid: '. . . but that does not mean that they must not do so'.

I hope that this careful analysis shows that while Susan can't be expected to choose to make what is important to her unimportant, she can be expected to choose between whether to keep her preference

Working with rigid and flexible attitudes 81

(that is, what is important to her) flexible or to make it rigid. This is illustrated in Figure 7.1.

When I encourage the client to make a choice between keeping their preferences flexible or making them rigid, I will help the person to understand the following points:

- a flexible attitude has two components: (1) a preference (what the person wants or what is important to them) and (2) an anti-rigid component (which states that the person does not have to get their preference met);
- a rigid attitude also has two components: (1) a preference (again what the person wants or what is important to them) and (2) a pro-rigid component (which states that the person does have to get their preference met).

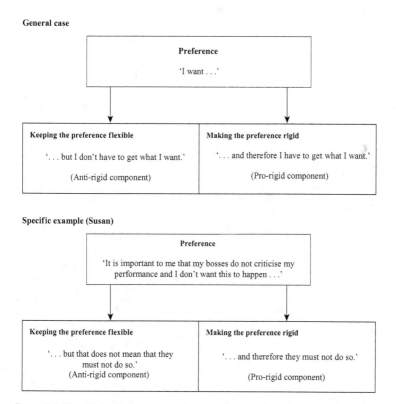

Figure 7.1 The choice between keeping a preference (or what is important) flexible or making it rigid

82 Working with rigid and flexible attitudes

In doing this work, it is often useful to use a visual aid as shown in Figure 7.1. This figure provides the general principle and an example taken from the case study of Susan used in this book.

7.3 Helping the client to choose between the two options: dialectical enquiry

The client now understands the difference between the two options. Their choice is either to hold the attitude where they acknowledge what they want and hold that they must get what they want (rigid attitude) or to hold the attitude where they acknowledge what they want and hold that they don't have to get what they want (flexible attitude). So the basic choice is to hold either the anti-rigid component or the pro-rigid component. This is again illustrated in Figure 7.1. I help the client choose by engaging them in a dialectical examination of both attitudes. As Chapter 9 will show, this is best done when my client and I have agreed a goal with respect to the client's problem.

Dialectical enquiry in FCBT involves my client and myself aiming to discover the truth, logical sense and best pragmatic outcome[3] concerning the client's attitudes. We do so through examining the opposing rigid and flexible attitudes that have already been identified and understood.

A choice-based examination of rigid vs flexible attitudes requires me to ask the client to stand back and consider both attitudes from a variety of standpoints, mainly the reality standpoint, the logical standpoint and the pragmatic standpoint. It is useful if the client can consider these two attitudes simultaneously, perhaps in written form, when I ask them a series of choice-based questions. In our example, I have written Susan's attitudes on a whiteboard as follows:

Rigid attitude (No. 1)	Flexible attitude (No. 2)
'It is important to me that my bosses do not criticise my performance and I don't want this to happen and therefore they must not do so.'	'It is important to me that my bosses do not criticise my performance and I don't want this to happen, but that does not mean that they must not do so.'

7.3.1 Choice-based examination of rigid vs flexible attitudes: the reality standpoint

In helping a client to consider both their rigid and flexible attitudes from the reality standpoint, I ask the client to consider how the world works

Working with rigid and flexible attitudes 83

in reality. Is the world obliged to grant them their preferences or not? Unfortunately, not! I helped Susan to see that however much she wanted her bosses not to criticise her, the world is not a place that would guarantee that this does not happen. Clients struggle with this idea, particularly when they consider themselves deserving of having their preferences met. When clients accept that the world is a place where they may get their preferences met, but not necessarily, is what I call a 'cod liver oil' moment.[4] Accepting that one does not have to have one's preferences met enables the client to focus on the adversity should this happen, face up to it and process it through the lens of their non-extreme attitudes, which will be discussed later.

7.3.2 Choice-based examination of rigid vs flexible attitudes: the logical sense standpoint

When I ask a client whether it makes sense to conclude that because they want something, it therefore follows that they don't have to get it, the client invariably says yes, but finds it difficult to come up with a reason that is different from the one above – that is, it is in accord with the way the world works. However, there is a logical argument that can be used that goes like this:

- A preference is a statement of fact. The client does hold it. In other words, it is an 'is' which I will call 'Is #1'.
- The anti-rigid component is also an 'is'. Thus, it is a fact that the person does not have to have their preference met. I will call this 'Is #2'.
- In logic, 'Is #2' follows logically from 'Is #1' since they are both facts that can be logically connected. Thus: I want x, and it is logical for me to conclude that I don't have to have it.
- Also, it is not logical to conclude that because I want something ('is') it follows that I have to have it ('ought'). In logic, one cannot derive an 'ought' from an 'is' (Hume's Law). In truth, most clients understand this logical argument, but are not moved by it.

Susan was prepared to accept that because she did not want her bosses to criticise her it did not make sense for her to conclude that they therefore must not do so, but, in truth, it was not particularly a 'lightbulb' moment for her.

7.3.3 Choice-based examination of rigid vs flexible attitudes: the pragmatic standpoint

Dr Phil, the psychologist and American television personality, host of the talk show *Dr Phil*, has a famous catchphrase, which is 'How's that working for you?' This is precisely the question that I ask the client with respect to both their rigid attitude and their flexible attitude. The client will mostly see that it is their flexible attitude that will best help them achieve their goals and objectives and it is the anti-rigid component of this attitude that allows the client to act on their preference in the healthiest way possible. They can see, in contrast, that their rigid attitude will only lead to emotional disturbance and will thwart their progress towards their goals.

Susan could see that her rigid attitude was the main reason she was anxious about speaking in front of her bosses, and that, by contrast, her flexible attitude would help her to be concerned, but not anxious, about the possibility of her bosses being critical of her performance.

7.3.4 Help the client to identify and respond to their doubts, reservations and objections (DROs) to adopting flexible attitudes and letting go of rigid attitudes

If I were to give you, the reader, a large stack of £20 notes with instructions to stand on a street corner and give one of the notes away to every passer-by, do you think that everyone would take one? The answer is 'no'. So why do people look a gift horse in the mouth? What reason would they give for not accepting the money? The following are some likely reasons: 'This is a scam'; 'If it seems too good to be true, it probably is'; 'I'll get into trouble if I take it.' In the same way, even though the client's flexible attitude represents how the world operates, makes sense and works for the person, they still may resist it and still cling to their rigid attitude. It is my job to be able to recognise this situation and help the client identify and respond to any doubts, reservations and objections (DROs) they may have towards adopting their flexible attitude and surrendering their rigid attitude. Here are some common client DROs on this issue and suggested responses to them:

- *DRO*: 'My flexible attitude won't motivate me as much as my rigid attitude.'

  Response: Your preference component is the motivating aspect of both attitudes, so they are both equally motivating. The anti-rigid

Working with rigid and flexible attitudes   85

component of the flexible attitude will allow you to act on your motivation free from the disturbing effect of the rigid component of the rigid attitude.

- *DRO*: 'My rigid attitude shows what is really important to me, while my flexible attitude fails to do this.'

  Response: The common preference component of both attitudes indicates level of importance and is of equal intensity in both. So, your flexible attitude does show what is important to you as much as your rigid attitude.

7.4 The importance of taking action in the face of adversity

If clients do not act in ways consistent with their flexible attitudes and if they do not do so while facing adversity, these attitudes will not take root and they will just understand them intellectually but they will not influence their behaviour, thinking and emotion. Such adversity facing attitudinal-behavioural consistency needs to be implemented frequently by the client. It is also useful if this action is first rehearsed in imagery before the actual behaviour is implemented.

When a client takes action, it is important that they rehearse their flexible attitudes in the face of adversity and that they do this in a way that is 'challenging, but not overwhelming' for them (Dryden, 1985). They also need to face adversity without the use of safety-seeking behaviour and thinking. These manoeuvres have the effect of preventing the client from processing the adversity with their developing flexible attitude and will weaken the extent of the progress the client will make. I will help the client to identify these safety-seeking manoeuvres and discuss with them ways of responding to such manoeuvres to limit their use. A common approach here is to help clients identify the urge to use the manoeuvre and to respond to these in ways resulting in healthier thinking and action instead. I discourage the client from attempting to abandon the urge, since such attempts will only have the paradoxical effect of strengthening it.

7.5 Helping clients to develop a flexible mindset

I will assume in this section, that I have helped the client deal with their emotional problem(s) by helping them develop flexible, non-extreme attitudes towards the adversities that embody the problem(s). It is

86 Working with rigid and flexible attitudes

best, in the way that I work, if developing a flexible mindset is based on developing a flexible attitude. As will be shown, a flexible mindset includes (1) being balanced in one's thinking; (2) being able to see things from different perspectives; (3) seeing exceptions; and (4) being pluralistic in outlook.

7.5.1 Help the client to be balanced and see a range of possible outcomes of their actions

When clients plan to take action either in life or as part of the therapy work they have agreed to undertake with me as their therapist, then, when they are asked to consider the possible outcomes of their actions, they will either be:

- optimistic and predict positive outcomes for their actions;
- pessimistic and predict negative outcomes for their actions;
- balanced and realistic and predict a mixture of positive and negative outcomes.

Although you may think that the optimistic position is the healthiest of the three, I would argue that the realistic position is the healthiest. This is for two reasons. First, this position is the most realistic of the three. There are very few client behaviours that will yield uniformly positive outcomes or uniformly negative outcomes. Client behaviours are more likely to result in some outcomes that are positive, some that are negative and some that are neutral. Second, this position gives the client an opportunity to prepare to deal with some of the negative outcomes they have predicted. If they only predict negative outcomes, they will be overwhelmed and will probably avoid dealing with any of these adversities.

This balanced, realistic approach also explains why I encourage my client to assume, for the time being, that the adversity that they have inferred at 'A' in the 'Situational ABC' framework is true, because it might well be (see Appendix).

7.5.2 Help the client to look at things from different perspectives

Being able to stand back and review things from different perspectives is a good sign that a client has a flexible mindset.

7.5.2.1 Looking at things from the different perspectives of involved individuals

A sign of a fixed mindset is when a client either cannot see other people's perspectives or thinks that others must view a situation as they view them. Encouraging them to put themselves into the shoes of each of the other people involved is vital. I will do this by asking the client questions such as: 'From what you know about this person, how do you think they saw this situation?' I ask the client to do this for every person involved.

7.5.2.2 Looking at things from different time perspectives

Some clients adopt a long-term perspective on their life, while others adopt a short-term perspective. Although both these perspectives have advantages, they also have disadvantages. Only taking a short-term perspective on life, for instance, means that a person gets a lot of short-term pleasure, but lacks any sense that they are pursuing the kind of longer-term meaningful goals that being committed to a longer-term perspective tends to bring. Conversely, only taking a long-term perspective means that the person will be striving towards important longer-term goals, but will derive little pleasure from life. When a client takes both a short-term and long-term perspective on their life they can have the best of both worlds. A feature of how I work is that I actively help my client adopt this dual time perspective.

7.5.3 Help the client to be mindful of exceptions

In my view, one of the chief characteristics of a flexible mindset is being able to look for and incorporate the existence of exceptions in one's thinking. This is an important aspect of the solutions approach to therapy (for instance, Iveson et al., 2012). When a client becomes aware that they have a problem it is quite easy for them to become fixed in the idea that this problem will always happen in the same situations in which it has occurred in the past. In these circumstances, I am inclined to ask the client to identify times in which the problem did not happen in situations when it was expected to happen and which constitute the exceptions to the problem. Such exceptions can then be explored so that the client may be helped to identify the factors involved in their non-problem response. These factors can then lead to a solution to the person's problem.

88 Working with rigid and flexible attitudes

7.5.4 Help the client to be pluralistic in their outlook and engagement

Pluralism has been defined as an active engagement with diversity, in all its forms, rather than the diversity itself (Eck, 2006). It is based on the ability of the client to recognise that people belonging to the same category are different from each other and that there is also diversity within each person. The client may respond differently to the same set of circumstances at different times. Therefore, the client with a flexible mindset can engage both with interpersonal and intrapersonal diversity. This engagement makes it possible for the client to construct and maintain a complex rather than simple understanding of self and others. One way that I promote client pluralism is to encourage clients to seek out unfamiliar situations they would not usually encounter and people with whom they would not ordinarily interact. This is to ensure that client pluralism is experientially rather than theoretically based.

Another way in which I help clients to be pluralistic in outlook is by encouraging them to use 'both/and' rather than 'either/or' thinking. This helps protect the client from viewing the world in simplistic, discrete categories and instead encourages them to develop flexible views for a complex world.

7.5.5 Help the client be flexible about uncertainty

When we have established certainty about an event (for instance, a diagnosis of a health problem), we either know that there is something wrong or that there is nothing wrong because we have just been given the diagnosis. When we are uncertain about the same event (i.e. we have not yet received the diagnosis), we don't know whether or not something is amiss. When the client is flexible about uncertainty in this situation, they can hold equally to the idea that there may or may not be something wrong and this helps them to tolerate the uncertainty.[5]

When the person lacks flexibility about uncertainty, they will tend to associate uncertainty with a negative outcome, as shown earlier in the chapter. In such cases, when faced with uncertainty, the person will assume that there is something wrong with them.

To summarise, uncertainty is an adversity to be tolerated and dealt with flexibly while the person is taking action to gain the desired knowledge.

7.5.6 Help the client benefit from the reciprocal influence of a flexible mindset and adaptability

The client's ability to react constructively to the changing nature of their environment is not only enhanced by a flexible mindset but itself enhances that mindset. Cognition and behaviour are interdependent processes in the way I work. That means that some of the time I will help the client to adapt behaviourally by first helping them develop a flexible attitude, particularly in the context of dealing with an emotional problem, while at other times, I will help the client develop behavioural adaptability knowing that doing so will also help them develop a flexible mindset.

In Chapter 8, I will discuss how I help clients to address a set of extreme attitudes and to develop and maintain an alternative set of non-extreme attitudes.

Chapter 8

Working with extreme and non-extreme attitudes in therapy

I will discuss in this chapter how I work with clients' extreme attitudes in order to help them develop healthy, realistic and sensible non-extreme attitudes. This work is again predicated on the premise that a client understands the role such attitudes play in their problems and their potential solutions and has modified the form and content of these attitudes in the assessment process with me as their therapist to reflect their specific problems. You should bear in mind throughout that according to the way I work, extreme and non-extreme attitudes are derived from the rigid and flexible attitudes that lie at the core of psychological disturbance and health respectively.

I agree with my REBT colleagues that three major extreme attitudes are derived from rigid attitudes and three major non-extreme attitudes are derived from flexible attitudes. I will discuss both extreme and non-extreme attitudes in the order as shown in Table 8.1, which shows both sets.

Table 8.1 Extreme and non-extreme attitudes derived from rigid and flexible attitudes respectively

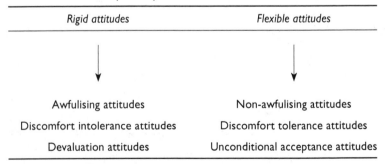

8.1 The emphasis of choice in the awfulising and non-awfulising attitudes taken towards adversities

When the client is facing an adversity, they have the choice of adopting an awfulising attitude or a non-awfulising attitude towards it.

8.1.1 Helping the client to see the difference between awfulising and non-awfulising attitudes

In working with a client's extreme awfulising and non-extreme non-awfulising attitudes the first stage is to help them see clearly the difference between the two. In doing so, I will help the client to understand that both attitudes are based on a negative evaluation of adversity.

8.1.1.1 Characteristics of an awfulising attitude

When a person holds an awfulising attitude, they mean that:

- nothing could be worse;
- the event in question is worse than 100% bad;
- no good could possibly come from this bad event as it is completely bad;
- the event cannot be transcended.

8.1.1.2 Characteristics of a non-awfulising attitude

When a person holds a non-awfulising attitude, they mean that:

- things could always be worse;
- the event in question is less than 100% bad;
- good things could come from this bad event;
- the event can be transcended.

8.1.2 Negative evaluations: not a target for change in therapy

When a client has a problem for which they seek help, I assume that they are facing an adversity they evaluate negatively. This is the case whether the person is disturbed about the adversity involved in the

92 Extreme and non-extreme attitudes

problem or whether they respond constructively to the adversity. I shall again take the example of Susan, who came to therapy for help with her public-speaking anxiety. In the specific episode that she and I chose to focus on, Susan was anxious about her performance being criticised by her bosses who would be at her presentation. So let us review what we know, which is that, given Susan's preference for her bosses not to be critical of her, Susan would evaluate this adversity negatively should this happen. Such a negative evaluation is not a target for change since it would neither be realistic nor healthy for Susan to evaluate this adversity positively or neutrally. If I do not encourage the client to change their negative evaluation of the adversity, then the object of change lies elsewhere. It lies with the two ways in which people deal with their negative evaluations.

8.1.3 The choice: keeping awful out of badness vs adding awful to badness

We have just seen that a negative evaluation of an adversity (i.e. when a client's preference is not met) is common to both psychological disturbance and psychological health. The distinction between disturbance and health is whether a person can keep that negative evaluation non-extreme or whether they make it extreme. In Susan's case, her disturbance-promoting extreme awfulising attitude begins with a negative evaluation: 'It would be bad if my bosses criticise my performance . . .' and then ends with a statement that makes it clear she has made her evaluation extreme: '. . . and therefore it would be awful'. Compare this with what could be Susan's health-promoting non-extreme, non-awfulising attitude. Note that this too starts with the same negative evaluation: 'It would be bad if my bosses criticise my performance . . .' and then ends with a statement that makes it clear that she has kept her evaluation non-extreme: '. . . but it would not be awful'.

This careful analysis shows, it is to be hoped, that while Susan can't be expected to choose to change her negative evaluation of the adversity, she can be expected to choose between whether to keep her negative evaluation non-extreme or make it extreme, as is shown in Figure 8.1.

In encouraging the client to make a choice between keeping their negative evaluation non-extreme (non-awfulising) or making it extreme (awfulising), I will help the person to understand the following points:

Extreme and non-extreme attitudes 93

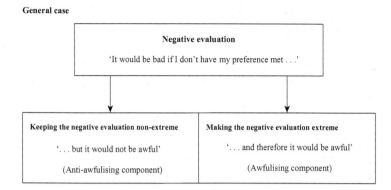

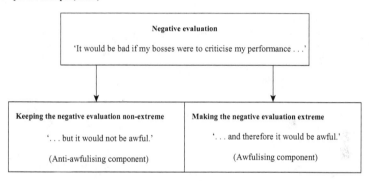

Figure 8.1 The choice between keeping a negative evaluation non-extreme or making it extreme

- A non-extreme, non-awfulising attitude has two components: (1) a negative evaluation (of the adversity that the person is facing) and (2) an anti-awfulising component (stating that it is not awful when the person faces the adversity).
- An extreme, awfulising attitude also has two components: (1) a negative evaluation (of the same adversity) and (2) an awfulising component (which states that it is awful when the person faces the adversity).

In undertaking this work, it is frequently useful to employ a visual aid as shown in Figure 8.1. This figure provides the general principle and an example taken from the case example of Susan used in this book.

94 Extreme and non-extreme attitudes

8.1.4 Helping the client to choose between the two options: dialectical enquiry

The client now understands the difference between the two options. Their choice is to maintain the attitude where they negatively evaluate the adversity and make that evaluation extreme (awfulising attitude) or to keep that evaluation non-extreme (non-awfulising attitude). The basic choice is to maintain the anti-awfulising component or the awfulising component, which is again shown in Figure 8.1. I help the client make the choice by engaging them in a dialectical examination of both attitudes. As noted in Chapter 7, this is best done when the client and I have agreed a goal concerning the client's problem.

As I have noted in Chapter 7, dialectical enquiry in FCBT involves the client and I aiming to discover the truth, logical sense and best pragmatic outcome concerning the client's attitudes by examining these opposing awfulising and non-awfulising attitudes that have already been identified and understood.

A choice-based examination of awfulising vs non-awfulising attitudes involves my asking the client to stand back and consider both attitudes from a variety of standpoints, mainly the reality standpoint, the logical standpoint and the pragmatic standpoint. It is useful to have a written representation of these two attitudes to view when I ask the client a series of choice-based questions about the attitudes. In our example, I wrote Susan's attitudes on a whiteboard as follows:

Awfulising attitude (No. 1)	Non-awfulising attitude (No. 2)
'It would be bad if my bosses were to criticise my performance and therefore it would be awful.'	'It would be bad if my bosses were to criticise my performance, but it would not be awful.'

8.1.5 Choice-based examination of awfulising vs non-awfulising attitudes: the reality standpoint

When helping a client to consider their awfulising and non-awfulising attitudes from the reality standpoint, the client is asked to consider the reality of how the world works. This is what I did with Susan who was helped to see that her non-awfulising attitude was consistent with reality and her awfulising attitude was inconsistent with reality. Thus, in the world:

1 Things could be worse for Susan than her bosses criticising her performance.
2 From this it follows that being criticised by her bosses is not 100% bad.

Extreme and non-extreme attitudes 95

3 Since Susan could learn something productive from being criticised by her bosses, it follows that the statement 'good can come from this event' is true.
4 This event can be transcended. No matter how bad being criticised by her bosses is, it is possible for Susan to process it and move on with her life.

8.1.6 Choice-based examination of awfulising vs non-awfulising attitudes: the logical sense standpoint

When the client says that it is bad to face an adversity and I ask them whether it is logical to conclude that it is awful to do so or not awful to do so, they tend to reply the latter, but find it difficult to come up with a reason. However, there is a logical argument that can be used which goes like this:

- A negative evaluation (for instance, 'It would be bad if my bosses criticised my performance . . .') is non-extreme.
- In an awfulising attitude the conclusion ('. . . therefore it would be awful') is extreme.
- In a non-awfulising attitude the conclusion ('. . . but it would not be awful') is non-extreme.
- Linking two non-extreme components is logical; therefore the non-awfulising attitude is logical.
- Deriving an extreme component from a non-extreme component is not logical; therefore the awfulising attitude is illogical.

Susan was prepared to accept that it was logical for her to conclude that it was not awful to be criticised by her bosses even thought it would be bad if this happened.

8.1.7 Choice-based examination of awfulising vs non-awfulising attitudes: the pragmatic standpoint

The client will see most of the time that it is their non-awfulising attitude that will best help them to achieve their goals and objectives and that their awfulising attitude will only lead to emotional disturbance and will thwart their progress towards their goals.

Susan could see that her awfulising attitude was closely related to her anxiety about speaking in front of her bosses and that even though part of her job was to make presentations her awfulising attitude would also lead her to avoid making presentations. She also saw that her non-awfulising

96 Extreme and non-extreme attitudes

attitude would, by contrast, help her to be concerned, but not anxious, about the possibility of her bosses being critical of her performance and that she would do the presentations rather than try to avoid them.

8.1.8 Help the client to identify and respond to their doubts, reservations and objections (DROs) to adopting non-awfulising attitudes and letting go of awfulising attitudes

As I noted in Chapter 7, my job as therapist is to help the client to identify and respond to any doubts, reservations and objections (DROs) they may have to adopting their non-awfulising attitude and letting go of their awfulising attitude. The following are some common client DROs on this issue and suggested responses to them:

- *DRO*: 'My awfulising attitude shows that what has happened to me is very bad while the non-awfulising attitude makes light of it. Therefore, by surrendering my awfulising attitude in favour of the non-awfulising alternative, I am making light of what is very bad about my life.'

  Response: Both attitudes incorporate the same evaluation of badness that 'it is very bad that the event occurred' and therefore neither of them make light of the event in question.

- *DRO*: 'My awfulising attitude sensibly protects me from threat, while my non-awfulising attitude needlessly exposes me to it.'

  Response: The healthiest way to deal with threat is to face it, process it properly and then respond to it constructively. Your awfulising attitude does not allow you to do that. So, although you are protected, it's not a healthy protection. The non-awfulising attitude will help you to 'face–process–respond' but at a time of your choosing so it's more a case of healthy, prepared exposure rather than 'needless' exposure.

8.1.9 The importance of taking action in the face of adversity

Note: The material in this section applies to the development of all three non-extreme attitudes: non-awfulising attitudes, discomfort tolerance attitudes and unconditional acceptance attitudes and as such, will not be repeated.

As I pointed out in Chapter 7, if clients do not act in ways consistent with their healthy non-extreme attitudes and if they do not do so while facing adversity, then these attitudes will not take root and will just be understood by them theoretically without influencing their behaviour, thinking and emotion. Such adversity facing attitudinal-behavioural consistency does need to be implemented frequently by the client. It is useful if such action is first rehearsed in imagery before the actual behaviour is implemented.

It is important when taking action that clients rehearse their non-extreme attitudes in the face of adversity and do this in a way that is challenging but not overwhelming for them (Dryden, 1985). It is also important that they face adversity without using safety-seeking behaviour and thinking. Such manoeuvres have the effect of preventing clients from processing the adversity with their developing non-extreme attitude and attenuating the amount of progress clients will make. I will help clients to identify such safety-seeking manoeuvres and will discuss with clients ways of responding to them to limit their use. A common approach here is to help clients identify the urge to use the manoeuvres and to respond to them in ways that result in healthier thinking and action. I discourage clients from making attempts to get rid of the urge, since such attempts will only have the paradoxical effect of strengthening it.

8.2 The emphasis of choice in the discomfort intolerance and discomfort tolerance attitudes held towards adversities

Clients facing an adversity have the choice of adopting a discomfort tolerance or discomfort intolerance attitude towards it.

8.2.1 Helping the client to see the difference between discomfort intolerance and discomfort tolerance attitudes

The first stage in working with a client's extreme discomfort intolerance and non-extreme discomfort tolerance attitudes is helping them to see clearly the difference between the two. In doing so, I help the client understand that both attitudes are based on a sense of struggle in dealing with the adversity.

98 Extreme and non-extreme attitudes

8.2.1.1 Characteristics of a discomfort intolerance attitude

When a person holds a discomfort intolerance attitude, they believe that:

- they will die or disintegrate if the adversity continues to exist;
- they will lose the capacity to experience happiness if the adversity continues to exist.

8.2.1.2 Characteristics of a discomfort tolerance attitude

When a person holds a discomfort tolerance attitude, they believe that:

- they will struggle if the adversity continues to exist, but that they will neither die nor disintegrate;
- they will not lose the capacity to experience some happiness if the adversity continues to exist, although this capacity will be temporarily compromised;
- the discomfort is worth tolerating, all things considered;
- they are willing to tolerate the discomfort;
- they are going to tolerate the discomfort.

8.2.2 Struggle: not a target for change in therapy

When a person has a problem for which they seek help, I assume they are facing an adversity with which they are struggling. This is the case whether the person is disturbed about the adversity involved in the problem or whether they respond to the adversity constructively. Let's take the example once more of Susan who came to therapy for help with public-speaking anxiety. In the specific episode that she and I chose to focus on, Susan was anxious about her performance being criticised by her bosses who would be at her presentation. So, what do we know? We know that given Susan's preference for her bosses not to be critical of her, Susan would struggle in dealing with this adversity should this happen. Since it would be unrealistic and unhealthy for Susan not to struggle with the adversity, this sense of struggle is not a target for change. If I do not discourage the client from struggling with the adversity, the object of change lies elsewhere. It lies with the two ways in which people deal with their struggle.

8.2.3 The choice: turning the struggle into discomfort intolerance vs tolerating the struggle

Struggling to deal with an adversity (i.e. when a client's preference is not met), as we have just seen, is common both to psychological disturbance and psychological health. What distinguishes between disturbance and health, in the way I work, is whether a person thinks that they can tolerate the struggle or whether they think they can't tolerate the struggle. In Susan's case, her disturbance-promoting extreme, discomfort intolerance attitude begins with a sense of struggle: 'If my bosses criticise my performance it would be a struggle for me to bear it...' and then ends with an extreme statement '... and therefore I could not bear it.' Compare this with what could be Susan's health-promoting, non-extreme discomfort tolerance attitude. Note that this too begins the

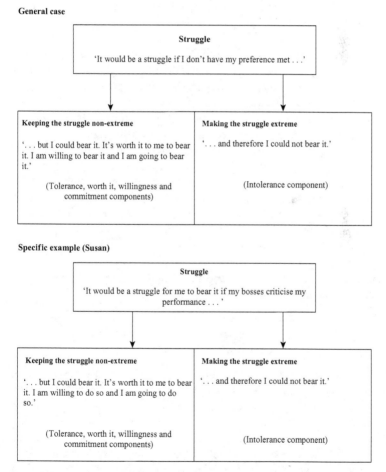

Figure 8.2 The choice between keeping struggle non-extreme or making it extreme

100 Extreme and non-extreme attitudes

same sense of struggle: 'If my bosses criticise my performance it would be a struggle for me to bear it . . .' and then ends with a non-extreme statement that makes several points clear: '. . . but I could bear it. It's worth it to me to bear it. I am willing to do so and I am going to do so.'

This careful analysis shows, it is to be hoped, that while Susan can't be expected to choose not to struggle to deal with the adversity, she can be expected to choose between whether to tolerate the struggle or not, which is shown in Figure 8.2.

When I encourage the client to make a choice between keeping their struggle non-extreme (discomfort tolerance) or making it extreme (discomfort intolerance), I will help the person to understand the following points:

- A non-extreme, discomfort tolerance attitude has five components: (1) a sense of struggle (in the face of the adversity the person is facing); (2) a tolerance component (which states that the person maintains that they can bear the discomfort of struggling); (3) a worth it component (which states that it is worth it for the person to tolerate the discomfort – if it is); (4) a willingness component (which states that the person is willing to tolerate the discomfort); and (5) a commitment component (which states that the person is going to tolerate the discomfort).
- An extreme, discomfort intolerance attitude has two components: (1) a sense of struggle (in the face of the same adversity) and (2) an intolerance component (which states that the person holds that they can't bear the discomfort of struggling).

I often use a visual aid in doing this work, as shown in Figure 8.2, which provides the general principle and an example taken from the case example of Susan used in this book.

8.2.4 Helping the client to choose between the two options: dialectical enquiry

The client now understands the difference between the two options. Their choice is to struggle in the face of the adversity and either think they can tolerate it etc. or that they can't tolerate it, which again is shown in Figure 8.2. I help the client make the choice by engaging them in a dialectical examination of both attitudes. As I noted in Chapter 7, this is best done when the client and I have agreed a goal with respect to the client's problem.

Again, as noted in Chapter 7, dialectical enquiry in FCBT involves the client and me aiming to discover the truth, logical sense and best pragmatic outcome concerning the client's attitudes through examining the opposing discomfort intolerance and discomfort tolerance attitudes that have already been identified and understood.

A choice-based examination of discomfort intolerance vs discomfort tolerance attitudes involves my asking the client to stand back and consider both attitudes from a variety of standpoints, particularly the reality standpoint, the logical standpoint and the pragmatic standpoint. As already noted having a written representation of these two attitudes to view is useful when the therapist asks the client a series of choice-based questions. In our example, I wrote Susan's attitudes on a whiteboard as follows:

Discomfort intolerance attitude (No. 1)	Discomfort tolerance attitude (No. 2)
'It would be a struggle for me to bear it if my bosses criticise my performance . . . and therefore I could not bear it.'	'It would be a struggle for me to bear it if my bosses criticise my performance . . . but I could bear it. It's worth it to me to bear it. I am willing to do so and I am going to do so.'

8.2.5 Choice-based examination of discomfort intolerance vs discomfort tolerance: the reality standpoint

The client is asked to consider the reality of how the world works in helping a client to consider their discomfort intolerance and discomfort tolerance attitudes from the reality standpoint. I did this with Susan who was helped to see that her discomfort tolerance attitude was consistent with reality and her discomfort tolerance attitude was inconsistent with reality. Thus, Susan could see that if her bosses did criticise her, she would struggle, but not disintegrate; she would be unhappy for a while, but would not forfeit the chance of happiness forever and that it would be worth it for her to tolerate it as this was the way to develop resilience. The world also allowed her to be willing and committed to tolerate this adversity and this was part of her personal repertoire of coping.

8.2.6 Choice-based examination of discomfort intolerance vs discomfort tolerance attitudes: the logical sense standpoint

When the client says that it is a struggle to deal with an adversity and I ask them whether it is logical to conclude that they can or cannot tolerate doing so, they tend to reply the latter, but find it difficult to come up with

102 Extreme and non-extreme attitudes

a reason. However, there is a logical argument that can be used, which is as follows:

- A sense of struggle (e.g. 'It would be a struggle for me to bear it if my bosses criticise my performance . . .') is non-extreme.
- In a discomfort intolerance attitude the conclusion '. . . and therefore I could not bear it' is extreme.
- In a non-awfulising attitude the conclusion '. . . but I could bear it – it's worth it to me to bear it, I am willing to do so and I am going to do so' is non-extreme.
- It is logical to link two non-extreme components; therefore the discomfort tolerance attitude is logical.
- It is not logical to derive an extreme component from a non-extreme component; therefore the discomfort intolerance attitude is illogical.

Susan was prepared to accept that it was logical for her to conclude that she could tolerate being criticised by her bosses for her performance even though she found doing so a struggle.

8.2.7 Choice-based examination of discomfort intolerance vs discomfort tolerance attitudes: the pragmatic standpoint

The client will see most of the time that it is their discomfort tolerance attitude that will help them best to achieve their goals and objectives and that their discomfort tolerance attitude will only lead to emotional disturbance and will thwart their progress towards their goals.

Susan could see that her discomfort intolerance attitude was closely related to her anxiety about speaking in front of her bosses and that it would also lead her to avoid making presentations even though it was part of her job to do so. She also saw that, by contrast, her discomfort tolerance would help her to be concerned, but not anxious, about the possibility of her bosses being critical of her performance and help her to continue giving presentations.

8.2.8 Help the client to identify and respond to their doubts, reservations and objections (DROs) to adopting discomfort tolerance attitudes and letting go of discomfort intolerance attitudes

As I have noted in Chapter 7, it is my job to help the client to identify and respond to any doubts, reservations and objections (DROs) they may have regarding adopting their discomfort tolerance attitude and letting go of their discomfort intolerance attitude. Here are some common client DROs on this issue and suggested responses to them:

- *DRO*: 'If I adopt my discomfort tolerance attitude, it means putting up with an adversity. My discomfort intolerance attitude discourages me from putting up with this situation.'

  Response: 'Putting up' with implies that you will do nothing to change the adversity. This is not the purpose of a discomfort tolerance attitude. Rather, its purpose is to help you face the adversity, change it if it can be changed and adjust constructively to it if it cannot. Your discomfort intolerance attitude will lead you to avoid the adversity, which means that you will neither change it nor adjust constructively to it. Such an attitude only results in problem maintenance.

- *DRO*: 'My discomfort intolerance attitude helps me to avoid emotional pain, while my discomfort tolerance attitude will expose me to more emotional pain. Therefore, I am reluctant to adopt a discomfort tolerance attitude.'

  Response: One of the major reasons why people unwittingly maintain their problems has been shown to be distress intolerance. Painful emotions exist to alert you to the fact that there is a problem to address and developing a discomfort tolerance attitude to your distress will allow you to do this. It is true that your discomfort intolerance attitude will lead you to take action to avoid emotional pain but this will result in problem maintenance. Avoiding distress means that you do not deal with the problem, whose presence is indicated by your emotional pain. In addition, being intolerant of emotional pain only results in an increase in the intensity of this pain if it cannot be avoided.

8.3 The emphasis of choice in the devaluation and unconditional acceptance attitudes held towards adversities

When the client is facing an adversity, they have the choice to adopt a devaluation attitude or an unconditional acceptance towards it.

8.3.1 Helping the client to see the difference between devaluation and unconditional acceptance attitudes

In working with a client's extreme devaluation and non-extreme unconditional acceptance the first stage is to help them see the difference

104 Extreme and non-extreme attitudes

between the two clearly. In doing so, I will help the client understand that both attitudes are based on a negative evaluation of an aspect of self, other(s) or life.

8.3.1.1 Characteristics of a devaluation attitude

When a person holds a devaluation attitude, they mean that:

- a person (self or other) can legitimately be given a single global rating that defines their essence and the worth of a person is dependent upon conditions that change (for instance, my worth goes up when I do well and goes down when I don't do well);
- life can legitimately be given a single rating defining its essential nature; the value of life varies according to what happens within it (e.g. the value of the world goes up when something fair happens and goes down when something unfair happens);
- a person can be rated on the basis of one of their aspects and life can be rated on the basis of one of its aspects.

8.3.1.2 Characteristics of an unconditional acceptance attitude

When a person holds an unconditional acceptance attitude, they mean that:

- a person cannot legitimately be given a single global rating that defines their essence; their worth, as far as they have it, is not dependent upon conditions that change (for instance, my worth stays the same whether or not I do well);
- life cannot legitimately be given a single rating that defines its essential nature and the value of life does not vary according to what happens within it (for instance, whether fairness exists at any given time or not, the value of life stays the same);
- it makes sense to rate discrete aspects of a person and of life, but does not make sense to rate a person or life on the basis of these discrete aspects.

8.3.2 Negative evaluations of aspects of self/other/ life: not a target for change in therapy

When a person has a problem for which they seek help, I assume that they focus on an aspect of self/other/life which they evaluate negatively.

This is the case whether the person is disturbed about this aspect or whether they respond to the aspect constructively. Again, I will consider the example of Susan who came to therapy for help with public-speaking anxiety. In the specific episode that she and I chose to focus on, Susan was anxious about her performance being criticised by her bosses who would be at her presentation. On further assessment it transpired that if her bosses criticised her performance, Susan would negatively evaluate her own performance. This negative evaluation is not a target for change since it would not be healthy or realistic for Susan to evaluate her poor performance positively or neutrally. If I do not encourage the client to change their negative evaluation of an aspect of self/other/life, then the object of change lies elsewhere. It lies with the two ways in which people deal with such negative evaluations of aspects of self/others/life.

8.3.3 The choice: devaluing self/other/life vs unconditionally accepting self/other/life

A negative evaluation of an aspect of self/other/life, as we have just seen, is common to both psychological disturbance and psychological health. What distinguishes between disturbance and health, in the way I work, is whether, as a consequence of negatively evaluating the aspect, a person devalues self/other/life or unconditionally accepts self/other/life. In Susan's case, her disturbance-promoting extreme self-devaluing attitude begins with a negative evaluation of her performance: 'If my bosses criticise my performance, it proves I did not perform well and that is bad . . .' and then ends with a statement that makes it clear that she has devalued herself: '. . . and it would prove that I am a failure.'

Compare this with what could be Susan's health-promoting non-extreme unconditional self-acceptance attitude. Note that this too begins the same negative evaluation: 'If my bosses criticise my performance, it proves I did not perform well and that is bad . . .' and then ends with a statement that makes it clear that she has kept her attitude towards herself non-extreme: '. . . but it would not prove that I am a failure. It would prove that I am fallible.'

I hope this careful analysis shows that while Susan can't be expected to choose to change her negative evaluation of her poor performance, she can be expected to choose between whether to accept herself unconditionally or to devalue herself. This is illustrated in Figure 8.3.

When I encourage the client to choose between unconditionally accepting self/other/life (non-extreme option) or devaluing self/other/life (extreme option), I am helping the person to understand the following points:

General case

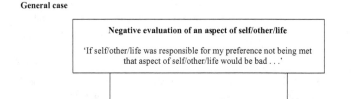

Specific example (Susan)

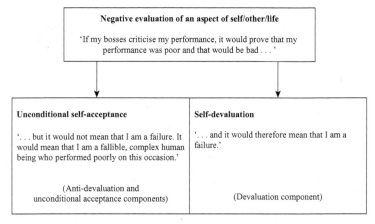

Figure 8.3 The choice between unconditional acceptance and devaluation attitudes

- A non-extreme, unconditional acceptance attitude has three components: (1) a negative evaluation of an aspect of self/other/life; (2) an anti-devaluation component (which states that the self/other/life cannot be legitimately devalued on the basis of the negative evaluation of the relevant aspect; and (3) an unconditional acceptance component (which states that self and other can be accepted for their complexity and fallibility and life can be accepted for its complexity).

- An extreme, devaluation attitude has two components: (1) a negative evaluation of an aspect of self/other/life; and (2) a devaluation of the whole of self/other/life.

In doing this work, it is often useful to use a visual aid as illustrated in Figure 8.3. This figure provides the general principle and an example taken from the case example of Susan used in this book.

8.3.4 Helping the client to choose between the two options: dialectical enquiry

The client now understands the difference between the two options. Their choice is, when they negatively evaluate an aspect of self/other/life, to hold a self/other/life devaluation attitude or an unconditional self/other/life acceptance attitude. This is again illustrated in Figure 8.3. I help the client to make the choice by engaging them in a dialectical examination of both attitudes. As I have noted in Chapter 7, this is best done when the client and I have agreed a goal concerning the client's problem.

Also as noted in Chapter 7, dialectical enquiry in FCBT involves the client and me aiming to discover the truth, logical sense and best pragmatic outcome concerning the client's attitudes through examining these opposing devaluation and unconditional acceptance attitudes that have already been identified and understood.

A choice-based examination of devaluation vs unconditional acceptance attitudes involves my asking the client to stand back and consider both attitudes from a variety of standpoints, and particularly the reality standpoint, the logical standpoint and the pragmatic standpoint. Having a written representation of these two attitudes to view is useful when I ask the client a series of choice-based questions about these attitudes. In our example, I wrote Susan's attitudes on a whiteboard as follows:

Depreciation attitude (No. 1)	Unconditional acceptance attitude (No. 2)
'If my bosses criticise my performance, it would prove that my performance was poor and that would be bad and it would therefore mean that I am a failure.'	'If my bosses criticise my performance, it would prove that my performance was poor and that would be bad, but it would not mean that I am a failure. It would mean that I am a fallible, complex human being who performed poorly on this occasion.'

108 Extreme and non-extreme attitudes

8.3.5 Choice-based examination of devaluation vs unconditional acceptance attitudes: the reality standpoint

In helping a client to consider their devaluation and unconditional acceptance attitudes from the reality standpoint, the client is asked to consider the reality of how the world works. This is what I did with Susan who was helped to see that her unconditional self-acceptance attitude was consistent with reality and that her self-devaluation attitude was inconsistent with reality. Susan can thus prove that she is a fallible human being who acted poorly and that if she was a failure then all she could do in life was to fail, which is false.

8.3.6 Choice-based examination of devaluation vs unconditional acceptance attitudes: the logical sense standpoint

When the client argues that self/other/life was responsible for their preference not being met and that that aspect of self/other/life is bad, I ask them whether it is logical to conclude that the whole of self/other/life is bad or not. The answer is 'not' and the reason is that evaluating the whole of self/other/life on the basis of a part of self/other/life involves making the part–whole error of logic. It is logical, on the contrary, for the whole of self/other/life to incorporate the relevant aspect.

Susan was prepared to accept that it was logical for her to conclude that her fallibility incorporated her poor performance and that she cannot logically be defined by that performance: it was not awful to be criticised by her bosses even though it would be bad if this happened.

8.3.7 Choice-based examination of devaluation vs unconditional acceptance attitudes: the pragmatic standpoint

The client most of the time will see that their unconditional acceptance attitude will best help them to achieve their goals and objectives and their devaluation attitude will only lead to emotional disturbance and will thwart their progress towards their goals.

Susan could see that her self-devaluation attitude was related closely to her anxiety about speaking in front of her bosses and that, even though it was part of her job to do so, it would also lead her to avoid making presentations. She also saw that by contrast her unconditional self-acceptance attitude would help her to be concerned, but not anxious, about the possibility of her bosses being critical of her performance and that she would do the presentations rather than try to avoid them.

8.3.8 Help the client to identify and respond to their doubts, reservations and objections (DROs) to adopting unconditional attitudes and letting go of devaluation attitudes

As I have noted in Chapter 7, it is my job to help the client to identify and respond to any doubts, reservations and objections (DROs) that they may have to adopting their unconditional acceptance attitude and letting go of their devaluation attitude. Here are some common client DROs on this issue and some suggested responses to them:

- *DRO*: 'Unconditional self-acceptance means that I don't need to change aspects of myself with which I am unhappy. Self-devaluation, on the other hand, motivates me to change. Thus, adopting an unconditional self-acceptance attitude discourages personal change, while keeping my self-devaluation attitude encourages such change.'

  Response: Once you accept yourself unconditionally you focus on what you don't like about yourself. This attitude will help you focus on changing these aspects without the interfering effects of self-devaluation, since a self-devaluation attitude creates emotional disturbance which, in turn, will lead to avoidance or denial, none of which will help you to change.

- *DRO*: 'By adopting an unconditional other-acceptance attitude I am condoning that person's bad behaviour. Devaluing that person shows that I am not condoning their behaviour.'

  Response: Both unconditional other-acceptance and other-devaluation attitudes involve your recognising that the other person has acted badly. Neither of these attitudes involves your condoning that behaviour. Thus, with an unconditional other-acceptance attitude, you accept the person, but do not condone their behaviour and with an other-devaluation attitude you devalue the person as well as their behaviour which you also do not condone. I would argue that the first attitude is healthier for all concerned than the second.

In Chapter 9, the final chapter, I will discuss the process of therapy from the perspective of how I work, from its inception to its end.

Chapter 9

The change process in therapy

In discussing the change process in therapy from the perspective of the way I work, it is useful to have recourse to a model of this change. There are a number of these change models in the literature, but perhaps a little unsurprisingly, I tend to use my own.

9.1 Dryden's (2011b) stage-based model of the FCBT process

My stage-based model of the therapy process consists of six stages, which I will briefly outline before going on to discuss them more fully, one at a time. In doing so, I will emphasise how working alliance theory can influence the therapy at each stage.

The six stages in my model are briefly as follows:

1   Engagement
2   Exploration
3   Cognitive-experiential understanding
4   Change based on cognitive-experiential understanding
5   Working through
6   Ending

9.2 Engagement

As mentioned in Chapter 3, when someone first contacts me for help, they are in the applicant role rather than the client role. The person applying for help is, in my experience, seeking answers to the following questions, even though implicitly.

The change process in therapy | | |

9.2.1 Is the help that Windy Dryden has to offer me, the help that I need?

This issue can be said to be related to the views, goals and task domains of the working alliance. A client thus needs to have an understanding of how I work (*views*), have a sense of what this implies for what both they and I are going to do in therapy (*tasks*), and understand how all this is going to help them in the ways they want to be helped (*goals*).

One of my initial *tasks* is therefore to explain what I have to offer the client and outline what the client needs to bring to the process so that we can make a joint, negotiated decision regarding whether or not the client may find this process helpful.

9.2.2 Am I going to get along with Windy Dryden and is he the best person to help me?

These two issues focus on the *bond* domain of the working alliance. At the very first point of contact with me, a potential client is determining how I respond to them. I therefore need to pay attention to how I speak to a potential client on the phone and how I greet them when I first meet them. Generally, the potential client wants to know if they can get on with me and if I am going to offer the client a professional service, while it is my initial task to attend to these *bond* components of the alliance. When a person becomes a 'client' and we can both proceed to explore the client's concerns, the following conditions will have been met: (1) the person has made a negotiated decision to proceed based on their initial judgement that I can be helpful to them; (2) they feel comfortable enough to work with me; (3) they can agree with my practical terms including my confidentiality policy.

9.3 Exploration

As therapist one of my earliest *tasks* is to create a climate in which a client can feel free enough to disclose their problems for which they are seeking help. Creating this climate of safety can best be seen as facilitating work in the *bond* domain of the working alliance. As soon as a client feels free to disclose their problems, I can begin to help them explore these concerns. The crucial tasks at this stage of any approach to therapy are encouraging them to talk in their own way and communicating empathic understanding of what they are saying.

112   The change process in therapy

These are sometimes downplayed in CBT approaches, but not in the way I work. In a research-based review, Beutler et al. (2004) showed that therapist empathy encourages clients to explore their problems at a core level, but it is important that this exploration be paced so that, rather than feel threatened by the engagement, the client feels safe to engage in this exploration. Too much empathy too soon is problematic.

Following an initial open-ended exploratory phase, I will help the client to explore their problems in a more structured way using, for instance, the ABC framework outlined in the Appendix. This can be done explicitly, for example, by using a written ABC framework on a whiteboard or more implicitly. However, being pluralistic, I will also seek and include the client's views about how best to understand their problems. In addition, I will help the client to set problem-related goals so that we both know where we are heading. I will again use the ABC framework to do this either implicitly or explicitly and will once again be guided by the client's views on this point. The importance of the client dealing with adversity in problem-focused and goal-directed therapeutic discussions is one issue that I do emphasise during goal-setting.

Here are a few more questions a client may ask themselves during this period of exploration, albeit implicitly.

9.3.1 Does Windy Dryden understand me?

Among others, Egan (2014) has written about 'accurate' empathy. This term reflects not only my attempts to understand the client from their frame of reference, but how accurate I am in doing so. Although a client will not generally expect me to be accurate in all of my attempts to understand them, they will conclude that I am not sufficiently understanding of their concerns if I often fail to understand them from their point of view. This is unlikely to happen, however, with my pluralistically based emphasis on privileging the client's view, as even the client and I have different understandings. In this case, I endeavour to ensure that the client 'feels' understood from their perspective and I keep my own, different understanding as a hypothesis awaiting later confirmation or disconfirmation. If I am going to express my *view* here, I stress that I may be incorrect in this *view* and that I am happy to be proven wrong. If I try at this point to push this different understanding on to the client then the client may 'feel' misunderstood' and may reject FCBT at this early stage.

9.3.2 Do I feel comfortable exploring my problems with Windy Dryden?

The client, during the exploration phase, will get a sense of how comfortable they are in exploring their problems with me as therapist. If they are not sufficiently comfortable they may well terminate therapy prematurely. To guard against this, I will consider the following points.

9.3.2.1 Convey interest

Whether or not I am interested in the client is something they will soon sense. Common signs that I am interested in my client include: showing that I am listening attentively; getting basic information about the client right; and remembering key points about the client's life.

9.3.2.2 Ensure that the environment is conducive to therapy

- It is very important for the client to feel safe at the outset of therapy and the environment in which therapy takes place needs to reflect this. I therefore work in an environment free from outside interruption and I ensure that external noise does not intrude into therapy sessions. The environment in which the therapist works needs to reflect the fact that privacy is crucial to therapy.

9.3.2.3 Demonstrate good basic counselling skills

In my initial training, which was in counselling, great emphasis was placed on the acquisition and development of good basic counselling skills. This issue often receives lip service in CBT approaches, but is one of the foundations of how I work. Demonstrating these skills helps the client to feel comfortable enough to open up to me. By basic counselling skills I mean the following:

- *Attending* to what the client says in a way that demonstrates my presence, but without overwhelming the client. I express this by my non-verbal demeanour.
- *Listening* carefully to what the client says. Again, this is best demonstrated non-verbally.
- *Checking one's understanding.* I convey this by my wish to show that I have understood what the client has been saying. I try to convey a spirit of 'Have I got this right?' to the client who gets the sense that I am really interested in understanding them.

114 The change process in therapy

- *Questioning.* I ask questions for specific purposes and these are made transparent to and agreed with the client.
- *Summarising.* I sum up what the client and I have discussed so that we can agree on this and then explore further.
- *Effective communication skills.* It is really important for me to demonstrate a range of effective communication skills including: speaking clearly and at a rate that encourages the client to process information properly, prompting the person to talk, being concise in what I say and clarifying what I say.

9.3.3 Does Windy Dryden have sufficient expertise to help me?

As I mentioned in Chapter 2, some clients are more concerned with my expertise than whether or not they like me. These clients will tend to disclose themselves more fully if they regard me as knowledgeable and expert. Although it is important that I do not claim knowledge and expertise that I do not have, it is quite legitimate for me to capitalise on the knowledge and expertise I do have with such clients. I do this by (1) emphasising my qualifications; (2) making my consulting room look as professional as possible; (3) quoting the research literature; (4) recommending and referring to my writings.

9.4 Cognitive-experiential understanding

By cognitive understanding, I mean that the client understands that their problems are underpinned by rigid, extreme attitudes and that their problem-related goals can be achieved by developing and holding flexible, non-extreme attitudes. This understanding, however, is theoretical in nature and at this stage the level of their conviction in the flexible, non-extreme attitudes is not sufficient to promote emotional and behavioural change. By cognitive-experiential understanding, I mean that the client has a deep conviction in their flexible, non-extreme attitudes to the extent that it promotes emotional and behavioural change.

One purpose of therapy is to foster in the client a new understanding of self, others and the world, particularly – but not exclusively – regarding the problems for which the client has sought therapy. I argue that while cognitive understanding is important it is not enough to promote meaningful change. For change to be meaningful, understanding has to have both cognitive and emotional-experiential components. However, according to the way I work, cognitive understanding in most cases precedes cognitive-experiential understanding and it is legitimate for me to promote the former before the latter. Cognitive-experiential understanding is promoted mainly by the consistent application of cognitive, emotive and behavioural methods used in concert. Such understanding, in my view, is more likely to happen between sessions than within sessions by the execution of homework tasks.

9.4.1 Cognitive-experiential understanding and between-session work: the importance of negotiated homework tasks

The major purpose of homework tasks in the way I work is to help clients to deepen their conviction in their developing flexible, non-extreme attitudes, although, of course, such tasks can be carried out for other reasons, particularly those determined by the clients themselves.

9.4.1.1 Negotiating homework tasks

In negotiating homework tasks with the client, I endeavour to:

- ensure that my client and I have sufficient time to negotiate a suitable task at the end-of-therapy sessions;
- involve the client fully in the process and elicit and take seriously the client's own suggestions;
- ensure that the homework task follows from the work that we have done in the therapy session; thus, the task involved may be a reading task, a cognitive task, an imagery task, a behavioural task or a combined task;
- agree with the client the purpose of the task and what the client hopes to achieve by doing it;
- ensure that it is a task the client has the capability of doing;
- ensure that it is a task that the client has the skills to do; if not, I will teach the client these skills, if possible;
- encourage the client to commit to doing the task and agree its frequency, and where and when they are going to do it;
- identify and problem-solve any anticipated obstacles to task execution;
- suggest that the client make a written note of the task and its purpose and that the note can easily be consulted.

9.4.1.2 Reviewing homework tasks

It is important that I review the client's experience of carrying out the agreed task at the beginning of the following therapy session, unless there

116 The change process in therapy

is a good reason not to do so (e.g. the client is in crisis with a different issue). Here are some important points that I consider as I do so.

- I check whether or not the client did the task as agreed.
- I focus on what the client learned from doing the task.
- I capitalise on the client's learning during the session and beyond.
- I discover if the client made any change to the agreed task and explore and discuss the reason for this change.
- I deal with any obstacles that accounted for an unproductive change to the agreed task.
- I remark on any productive changes to the agreed task.
- I explore the reason(s) carefully if the client did not do the task at all and identify and deal with the obstacles.
- I re-negotiate the task, if still relevant, so that the client can gain the experience of addressing the obstacle and doing the task.

The repeated nature of homework tasks – where the client integrates cognitive, emotive and behavioural aspects of such tasks, as noted above, best facilitates the development of cognitive-experiential understanding in therapy.

9.4.2 Cognitive-experiential understanding and in-session work

Although the client's between-session work is the most important way of facilitating their cognitive-experiential understanding in therapy, there are a number of ways I can facilitate such understanding within sessions.

9.4.2.1 Help the client to use something that really resonates with them

During work to effect attitude change it helps to use something with which the client resonates as this will engage the client's emotions, which is an important ingredient in cognitive-experiential change. Although it is difficult for me to know what is going to resonate with the client, here are a few suggestions.

First, I listen carefully to the language the client uses in therapy sessions. If they often use certain words or phrases this may be one indication that such language is meaningful to them, particularly if it is accompanied by affect. The same applies to any recurrent imagery to which they may refer.

Second, I endeavour to notice whether the client demonstrates engagement with the language and concepts they use in therapy sessions. This engagement may be indicated by affect, an increase in attention, forward leaning and the repetition of language that I may use. Although the way I use any of this material will vary from client to client, its purpose is to provide a more affective climate so that cognitive understanding may become more experiential.

9.4.2.2 Structure interventions in ways that reflect how clients have been helped and have helped themselves in the past

Clients come to therapy with a history of self-help and of being helped and I routinely make enquiries about this history as part of their assessment procedure. I can then use these self-helping and helping principles to facilitate change with regard to the client's target problem.

9.4.2.3 Make use of the client's strengths

It is useful to know what the client's strengths are so that by referring to these strengths I can make their self-change efforts more meaningful and therefore more impactful.

9.4.2.4 Refer to the client's role model or to someone who has been influential in the client's life

One method of increasing the emotional impact of cognitive understanding is to link it to one of the client's role models and/or influential persons. This information can be obtained at the assessment stage or at this point in the therapy process. I may also suggest that the client keep this person in mind when putting into practice what they have learned in therapy sessions.

9.4.2.5 Utilise the client's learning style

The more of the client's learning style I can utilise (discovered at assessment or at this point in the process), the more likely is it that the client will derive affective benefit from cognitive understanding. The best way to discover this information is to ask the client directly.

9.4.2.5.1 UTILISE THE VISUAL MEDIUM AS WELL AS THE VERBAL MEDIUM

FCBT is correctly categorised as a talking therapy and therefore includes a lot of verbal communication between my client and myself. However, to enhance the impact of therapy, it is sometimes useful to use visual diagrams of verbal concepts, especially for those clients whose learning is enhanced by the visual medium. Figure 9.1 presents an example of such a diagram, which is known as the 'Big I–Little i' technique. It shows

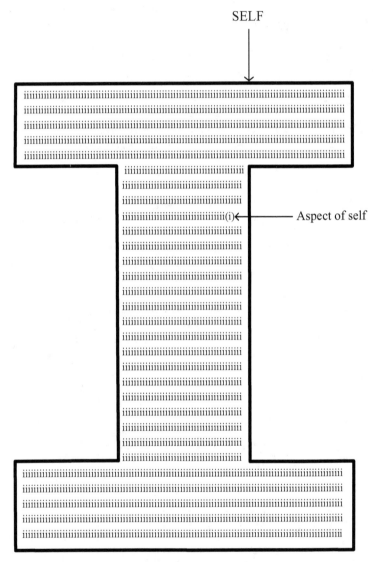

Figure 9.1 The Big I–Little i technique

The change process in therapy 119

that the 'Big I', representing a person, comprises a multitude of aspects represented by little 'i's. This shows that a person cannot be defined by any of their parts.

9.4.2.6 Refer to the client's core values to promote change

I have found discovering the client's core values at some point in the therapy process to be useful, especially when helping the person to see that such a value may reinforce a flexible and/or non-extreme attitude. In addition, a client may well endeavour to achieve a goal more persistently when it is underpinned by a core value than when it is not.

9.4.2.7 Use humour judiciously

The judicious use of humour in therapy may potentially be useful in helping to promote cognitive-experiential understanding. This is particularly the case when:

- clients show they have a sense of humour and in particular, can laugh at themselves;
- the humour is directed affectionately at some aspect of clients, but not the clients themselves;
- the humour has a therapeutic message that can be accurately articulated ideally by both my client and myself;
- that message can be used by the client in the service of their goals.

However, humour has the potential to be harmful and it is therefore important to seek and pay attention to the client's response and to seek feedback on its effect. I also ask the client at the outset whether my use of humour would be welcomed.

9.4.2.8 Consider using self-disclosure

Self-disclosure, like humour, is potentially very useful as a way of increasing the impact of interventions designed to promote cognitive-experiential understanding, but it is not universally welcomed by clients. Should I want to share a personal experience with a therapeutic message for the client, I will alert the client to that intention, and will ask for permission before doing so.

In my experience this self-disclosure therefore tends to be therapeutic when:

120 The change process in therapy

- it is wanted;
- it shows that I have had a similar problem, but am not ashamed about admitting it to myself and to others;
- the client 'feels' that the disclosure makes me equal to them in humanity;
- it clearly indicates what I did to deal constructively with the problem which may have relevance for the client. It therefore has a therapeutic point that the client may be able to utilise in addressing their target problem and in working towards their goals.

Even when the client has given permission for me to share my experience it is useful to get feedback concerning both its use and what the client has taken from the disclosure.

9.4.2.9 I Use a range of techniques to increase impact, but I construct my own

There are a multitude of techniques I can use to enhance client cognitive-experiential understanding (see Kellogg, 2015). I tend, however, to rely on my own creativity rather than on that of others in this area. Something may occur to me in my work with a client that may hit the spot. It may have never been used before and may never be used again. Given the specific context in which the bespoke intervention arose it is more likely to have an impact than when I use 'off-the-peg' techniques used by others that might be more relevant to particular clients. I find the bespoke rather than 'off-the-peg' use of imagery, metaphors and stories particularly important in this regard.

9.4.2.9.I HELP THE CLIENT TO DEVELOP A BRIEF, MEMORABLE, IMPACTFUL VERSION OF THEIR HEALTHY ATTITUDE

Among the challenges I face is how to help the client use a flexible and/or non-extreme attitude in the situation in which they need to use it, i.e. facing an adversity. As you will remember, I discussed flexible, non-extreme attitudes in Chapter 7. You will see, if you review that material, that both flexible and non-extreme beliefs tend to be wordy. To increase the impact of these attitudes and help the client use them when facing adversities, I endeavour to help clients to develop a version of the healthy attitude that reflects its meaning but that is brief, memorable and meaningful. I will then encourage clients to make a note of this statement and even to use it as a screensaver on their smartphone so that it can be quickly referred to when needed.

9.4.3 Cognitive-experiential understanding and working alliance theory

According to working alliance theory a number of things tend to take place in each of the four domains if progress towards cognitive-experiential understanding is to occur at this stage.

9.4.3.1 Cognitive-experiential understanding and bonds

As the client develops cognitive-experiential understanding, they tend to develop greater trust in me as their therapist, and are more likely to withstand difficulties in the relationship than in earlier stages, and benefit increasingly, where appropriate, from my expertise. Despite the rough patches common in therapy as clients struggle to change painful patterns while simultaneously holding on to them because they provide familiarity and predictability, the client and I have by now become used to one another and settled down into a productive working relationship.

9.4.3.2 Cognitive-experiential understanding and tasks

This productive relationship in the *task* domain is characterised by the client (1) developing a greater understanding of what they have to do in therapy and of what I am doing and (2) engaging more deeply in their tasks. Perhaps the greatest task for me is the timing of interventions. Going too slowly stretches the client insufficiently and the impetus of change may be lost. Going too fast too soon tends to engender resistance in the client as they are being asked to change too quickly with too little appreciation being taken of their defences. As Anna Freud (1946) showed many years ago, clients erect a number of psychological defences against change and when intervening in the *task* domain I take my clients' defences very much into account.

9.4.3.3 Cognitive-experiential understanding and views

My client and I share in the *views* domain a more sophisticated understanding of the former's difficulties and the relevant determinants of these difficulties. As the name of this stage makes clear, such understanding is experientially as well as cognitively understood by clients, and sets the stage for later changes to be made on the basis of this felt understanding. I begin with problem assessment and problem-based intervention, as I noted in Chapter 3, and construct a case formulation as therapy unfolds. As my client and I engage more deeply with the former's

122 The change process in therapy

problems, experiencing the successes and failures of doing so, the case formulation is enriched and deepens the client's level of conviction in their cognitive-experiential understanding.

9.4.3.4 Cognitive-experiential understanding and goals

Finally, in the *goals* domain of the alliance, the client and I will refine the former's goals according to a more sophisticated understanding of the client's problems generated at this stage. A client's goals sometimes do not alter throughout therapy, but they may sometimes change considerably. If I succeed in engaging clients in what I have called the 'reflection process' (see Chapter 2) and encourage them to understand that their goals may well change as therapy proceeds, then I will tend to be more helpful to the client than if I assume that, once negotiated at the outset, the client's goals will not alter.

In addition, when the work is going well at this stage, the client becomes increasingly sure about the relationship between what I am doing in the *task* domain and where they are heading in the *goals* domain.

9.5 Change based on cognitive-experiential understanding

Once clients have achieved a measure of cognitive-experiential understanding they need to capitalise on this and make changes. Such changes can be behavioural and/or philosophical in nature.

9.5.1 Behavioural change based on cognitive-experiential understanding

Although the stage-based model of the therapeutic process is intended to highlight broad differences of emphasis at each stage, it should not be thought that there is no overlap between what goes on between stages. This is particularly the case in considering the difference between the previous stage ('cognitive-experiential understanding') and this one, which focuses more on action taken on the basis of such understanding. For example, consider the point I made in the previous section about the difference between cognitive understanding and cognitive-experiential understanding. According to the way I work, one of the best ways to foster cognitive-experiential understanding is through action based on and consistent with cognitive understanding. New cognitive insights will remain theoretical without action. They will then be 'cognition without ignition'.

At this fourth stage major emphases are on refining the client's behavioural skills while teaching them new behavioural skills not currently in their repertoire. These skills include social skills for people who are shy and have not developed basic skills such as maintaining eye contact; assertion skills for those who have put others first or not developed the behavioural side of boundary setting; presentation skills for those who are nervous about public speaking; and test-taking skills for those who are anxious in examination settings.

As mentioned above, when the client acts on their new cognitive-experiential understanding they often tend to deepen this understanding. Thus, the work done at this stage often reinforces the gains made in the previous stage.

9.5.1.1 Encouraging the client to be aware of various guidelines for action and to choose well

When we are in a situation in which we need to take action, this action can be undertaken for different reasons. I encourage the client to make a list of guidelines to such action to facilitate their choice. Here are some common guidelines for action:

- *Comfort-oriented action.* Here, the client takes action to gain a sense of immediate comfort. When this conflicts with goal-directed action, the therapist needs to help the client focus on this issue and invite them to look at ways of responding when they have the urge to 'comfort act'.
- *Goal-directed action.* Here, action is taken by the person towards goals set with their therapist.
- *Habitual action.* Here, the client takes action based on habit. When this behaviour is self-defeating, the client can be helped to identify the beginning of the behaviour or the urge to act that goes along with the behaviour and to learn to go against the grain and to stop and see what their choices are.
- *Healthy attitude-based action.* Here, the client takes action to strengthen their conviction in a healthy attitude that they wish to develop.
- *Healthy body-based action.* Here, the client takes action to develop a healthy body which complements the above guideline.
- *Action to please others.* Here, clients take action to please others rather than themselves.

- *Value-based action.* Here, clients take action underpinned by one or more important values.
- *Commitment-based action.* Here, clients take action in line with a prior commitment they have made, either to themselves or to others.

From a therapeutic perspective, the more that client action is (1) consistent with developing a healthy attitude; (2) guided by a healthy goal; (3) underpinned by an important value and in line with a commitment made to others who are on one's team as well as to self, the more that action has the power to lead to change and to deepen the client's cognitive-experiential understanding.

9.5.2 Philosophical change based on cognitive-experiential understanding

Sometimes it happens that acting differently is not relevant to a client's problems. For instance, a client's emotional problems may relate to past behaviour (for example, guilt or shame), or it could be the case that acting differently is not going to change the adversity the client is facing (for instance, an incurable illness). The famous serenity prayer states: 'God grant me the serenity to accept the things I cannot change; courage to change the things I can; and wisdom to know the difference.' At this stage of therapy, I need to help the client develop (1) the wisdom to know that they need to make what I call here 'philosophical change' (by which I mean a fundamental change in outlook) without reference to behavioural change; and (2) the serenity to do this.

I agree with my REBT colleagues that it is possible to teach clients about the concepts of unconditional self-acceptance (USA) and unconditional life-acceptance (ULA) and show them specifically how to accept themselves for their past behaviour (Dryden, 1999a), and how to accept grim reality when they cannot change what they may wish to change.

My own approach in promoting such philosophical change is to encourage clients to engage in a dialogue between the part of themselves that is to do the accepting and the part of them resisting such acceptance. This is done through transformational chairwork (Kellogg, 2015). I will then encourage the client to identify residual blocks to this acceptance and help them respond to these blocks. This usually involves identifying and responding to one or more misconceptions about the concept of acceptance itself or what it might lead to. I encourage the client, if they agree, to go public with their new accepting outlook, since doing so often leads to others being supportive and reinforcing of their new philosophy.

Finally, I want to make the point that while I have considered behavioural change and philosophical change separately, they can in reality occur together.

9.5.2 Cognitive-experiential understanding and when to use a change-based focus (CBF) and when to use an acceptance-based focus (ABF) when dealing with thinking

One of the major recent developments within the broad tradition of cognitive behaviour therapy has been the growth of those CBT approaches that recommend clients to mindfully accept the presence of dysfunctional cognitions and troublesome feelings without engaging with them. This may be thought of as an acceptance-based focus (ABF) and is typical of what has become known as 'third-wave CBT'.

Generally, I recommend that clients identify, examine and change rigid, extreme attitudes (at 'B') in the ABC framework, while responding to distorted inferences (either at 'A' or at 'C'). In brief, I recommend that clients mindfully engage with troublesome cognitions (that is, inferences and attitudes) in order to change them. This may be known as a change-based focus (CBF).

However, I do use both foci in how I work. Here is how I make use of both a change-based focus (CBF), where inferences and attitudes are targeted for change and an acceptance-based focus (ABF) where these cognitions are mindfully accepted. Using the most appropriate focus can help the client both to capitalise on cognitive-experiential understanding and to deepen this understanding.

- When encouraging the client to engage dialectically with their rigid, extreme attitudes in the first instance I use a change-based focus (CBF). When the client considers on any particular occasion that they have got enough out of this focus as they can, I encourage them to shift to an acceptance-based focus (ABF) if the rigid and/or extreme attitudes are still in their mind. It is unrealistic to expect a person to be fully convinced of their CBF interventions in any single disputing episode.
- With highly distorted cognitive consequences of rigid, extreme attitudes, I teach the client to understand why these thoughts are so distorted (i.e. they are the product of rigid, extreme attitudes). Then, I help them to use the presence of these thoughts to identify the rigid, extreme attitudes that have spawned them and then to use

a change-based focus (CBF) with these attitudes. The therapist may then help the client use the same change-based focus to respond to these cognitive Cs, but to recognise that these thoughts may still reverberate in their mind, at which point the therapist can encourage them to switch to an acceptance-based focus (ABF). Such reverberation is a natural process as the mind does not switch off from such thoughts just because CBF methods have been successfully used on any one occasion.

As third-wave CBT therapists note, little productive change can be gained when clients get enmeshed and entwined with their rigid, extreme attitudes and distorted inferences and it is then that I use an acceptance-based focus (ABF). However, in my view, little can be gained by failing to encourage the client to respond constructively to these cognitions by employing a change-based focus (CBF) when they are able to do so.

9.6 Working through

Once a client has acted on their new cognitive-experiential understanding and/or developed a new constructive outlook on the adversities in their life that cannot be changed, they need to be helped to capitalise on their gains and be prepared to deal with lapses in order to avoid total relapse.

9.6.1 Helping the client to capitalise on their gains

It is a sad fact that most clients do not naturally generalise what they learn in therapy from one area of their lives to others. For example, I once helped a client deal with her need for her boss's approval to the extent that she was eventually able to assert herself constructively with her boss. She came in with a very similar issue a few sessions later: non-assertion for fear of incurring her friend's disapproval. Before I explored this issue with her, it emerged that while she could see the similarity between her need for the approval of both her friend and boss when it was pointed out to her, before the connection was put to her she had not been able to see it for herself. Moreover, she said that she did not think of generalising what she had learned about dealing with her boss's disapproval to dealing with her friend's disapproval.

This indicates that most clients need help to generalise their gains from one area to related areas. This is one of my chief tasks in the

The change process in therapy   127

working-through process. I address this task actively and will use the assessment of problems and case formulation I have developed with my client earlier in the therapy process, and modified as therapy proceeds, as a structured way of doing this.

9.6.2 Working with and anticipating lapses to prevent relapse

I acknowledge that when a client makes progress in therapy, they may experience lapses in their progress. A lapse is different from a relapse in the following regard. A lapse is a significant, but temporary, falling back along the road to recovery, but a relapse is a more fundamental, enduring return to the original problem state that prompted help-seeking in the first place. The two most important things I need to do at this stage of the therapy process are to (1) help the client learn from their lapses so that they don't become relapses; and (2) help them anticipate lapses so that they can learn to deal with the relevant factors before they lapse. I also help the client identify what may be called their vulnerability factors, namely, factors to which they are particularly vulnerable.

I tend to do this 'lapse work' in a structured but collaborative way, using tasks with which the client is likely to be familiar to help them identify and deal effectively with the situational, cognitive, emotive, behavioural and interpersonal factors that underpin the client's tendencies to lapse. Written diaries are therefore employed for identification purposes, and cognitive, behavioural and imagery techniques are used for intervention purposes. I elicit and incorporate, as elsewhere, the client's ideas concerning how to deal with lapses into their negotiated treatment plan.

9.6.3 Handing over the reins to the client

One of my final tasks during the working-through process involves helping clients to become their own therapists. When therapy is at its most effective, clients not only achieve their goals but take away from the process a way of helping themselves in the future based on what they have learned during therapy that they found particularly helpful. Thus, they may take away from therapy (1) the Situational ABC framework by which to identify and analyse their experiences, and (2) a range of specific techniques to employ when necessary.

9.7 Ending

The ending of a therapy relationship is often considered to be a difficult time for a client: it echoes their difficulties both in saying goodbye and in dealing with loss; and although I do not assume that ending is bound to be difficult for the client, due recognition should be given to the possibility that it may be so.

When ending therapy is considered to be difficult for a client then it is very important that I give due time to helping them deal with and work through their feelings about the ending of the therapy relationship. This applies particularly when the end of therapy has a definite final date. The reason I say this is that it is quite common for my client and I to negotiate a 'fading out' of therapy rather than set a definite end without this fading out occurring first. The fading approach to ending has the effect of diluting the importance of therapy's final end.

9.8 Some notes on dealing with 'obstacles to change'

Throughout this book I have attempted to show how working alliance theory can shed light on the process of how I work as a therapist. I have made clear those factors that tend to enhance therapy and those that tend to impede it. In this final chapter, it should be clear that there are many obstacles to progress in therapy and these can exist at all the stages of therapy I have discussed in this chapter.

9.8.1 Simple steps to dealing with obstacles to change

Although a thorough discussion of such obstacles and how to deal with them would require a separate volume (see Dryden & Neenan, 2011), what I do want to emphasise here is that I have discovered that for me the best way to deal with an obstacle is to follow a simple set of steps as follows:

1 Identifying the obstacle.
2 Agreeing with the client that it is an obstacle.
3 Encouraging the client to give their view of the obstacle.
4 Showing the client full respect even if they have largely contributed to the obstacle.
5 Showing empathy with the client concerning the difficulty of change.
6 Encouraging the client to stand back and reflect on the factors that contribute to the obstacle, and which need to be changed.

The change process in therapy   129

7   Acknowledging non-defensively when I am the obstacle and undertaking to change what I have been doing. Apologising to the client if necessary.
8   Helping the client to brainstorm ways of dealing with the factors that have contributed to the obstacle when I am not the source of the obstacle.
9   Helping the client evaluate possible ways of dealing with these factors and encouraging them to select the ones that seem most likely to be effective.
10 Evaluating the client's attempts to implement the above procedures.
11 Continuing with steps 8, 9 and 10 until the client has dealt with the obstacle to change.

To find out more about how to deal with threats to the working alliance across the therapy process, see Safran and Muran (2000).

9.8.2 Responding to a client's doubts, reservations and objections (DROs)

In Chapters 7 and 8, I discussed how I respond if the client demonstrates DROs to developing healthy flexible, non-extreme attitudes and letting go of rigid, extreme attitudes. When there is an obstacle to change in therapy, one factor I check is whether the client continues to hold such DROs concerning these attitudes or about any aspect of the therapeutic process. These matters, once discovered, should be referred to the reflection process and resolved there.

9.8.3 Detecting and dealing with a client's self-deception and excuses

The client will need to be honest with themselves and with me as therapist for the purpose of our alliance together to deal effectively with obstacles to change. However, given the natural human tendency to avoid sticky situations rather than face up to them, clients may make excuses and/or deceive themselves and me. This may be seen as an obstacle to dealing with obstacles! If the alliance between the client and myself is strong, however, I can encourage the client to reflect on the possibility that they are engaging in self- and other-deceit and excuse-making and help the client to discover tell-tale signs that this may be the case. The more I show compassion and understanding of the client for making excuses and deceiving both parties, the more likely the client will engage in an

130 The change process in therapy

exploration for the reasons for such defensive behaviour and deal with these reasons with me. Having achieved this, the two of us can return to dealing with the original obstacles to change by following the steps listed above.

We have reached the end of the book. I hope you have enjoyed it and that it has made you think about your own practice whatever approach to psychotherapy you practise. If you have any feedback, I would welcome hearing from you at windy@windydryden.com

Appendix

The models of psychological disturbance and health that I use in my work

I will discuss in this appendix the models of psychological disturbance and health that I use in my work. However, I will begin by explaining why I prefer the term 'attitude' to that of 'belief' as used in REBT, even though both are cognitions of appraisal that largely explain a person's psychological response to a meaningful event.

A.1 Attitude vs belief

REBT, as mentioned above, uses the term 'belief' to denote cognitive appraisal of a meaningful event that largely determines the person's psychological response to that event. The term 'belief' is problematic, however, because common conceptions of it are at variance with how the term is used in REBT theory. The term 'belief' has thus been defined by the *Oxford Dictionary of Psychology*, 4th edition (Colman, 2015) as 'any proposition that is accepted as true on the basis of inconclusive evidence'. A client may therefore say something like: 'I believe that you don't like me' and although they think that they have articulated a belief, this is not actually a belief as the term has been used in REBT, but rather an inference (see Chapter 6). It is very important, as we shall see, to distinguish between an inference at 'A' and an attitude (or belief as used in REBT) at 'B' and anything that will allow this distinction to be made routinely is to be welcomed.

Because of this ambiguity regarding the term 'belief', I decided to use the term 'attitude' in my work because it better describes the cognitive appraisal that is key to an understanding of psychological disturbance and health. Indeed, a study of definitions of the term 'attitude' reveals that it is closer to the meaning that REBT theorists

132 Appendix

ascribe to the term 'belief'. For instance, Colman (2015) defines attitude as 'an enduring pattern of evaluative responses towards a person, object, or issue'.

I realised that in deciding to use the term 'attitude' rather than the term 'belief', if I wanted to preserve the letter 'B' I needed to find a word beginning with 'B'. I therefore decided to employ the term 'Basic Attitudes'[1] when formally describing 'B' in the ABC framework that I use in my work. Although not ideal, this term includes 'attitudes' and indicates that they are central or *basic* in that they lie at the *base* of a person's responses to an adversity. Please note that I use the terms 'attitude' and 'basic attitude' interchangeably in this book.

A.2 The ABC model of psychological disturbance

I will present in this section the model of psychological disturbance I use in my work, which is expressed in an ABC framework (see the left-hand column in Table A.1).

Table A.1 The ABCs of psychological disturbance and health that I use in my work

Model of psychological disturbance	Model of psychological health
Situation	**Situation**
A = Adversity	**A = Adversity**
B = Basic attitudes (rigid and extreme)	**B = Basic attitudes** (flexible and non-extreme)

• Rigid attitudes (primary)
• Secondary extreme attitudes derived from rigid attitudes
 	
  o Awfulising attitudes
  o Discomfort intolerance attitudes
  o Devaluation attitudes (of self/others/life)
	• Flexible attitudes (primary)
	• Secondary non-extreme attitudes derived from flexible attitudes
	
	  o Non-awfulising attitudes
	  o Discomfort tolerance attitudes
	  o Unconditional acceptance attitudes of self/others/life

C = Consequences	**C = Consequences**
• Unhealthy negative emotion • Unconstructive behaviour • Highly distorted and ruminative thinking	• Healthy negative emotion • Constructive behaviour • Realistic, balanced and non-ruminative thinking

Appendix 133

'A'

'A' stands for 'adversity'. I use it to distinguish between something happening (situation) and what the person finds disturbing in that emotional episode (adversity).

'B'

'B' stands for 'basic attitudes'. As noted above, with respect to psychological disturbance and health, the term 'beliefs' is used in REBT, while I use the term 'basic attitudes' in my work. When they underpin a psychologically disturbed response to adversity, these basic attitudes are considered to be rigid and extreme. Of the two, rigid attitudes are considered to be at the core of psychological disturbance and extreme attitudes are considered to be derived from these rigid attitudes.

'C'

In the ABC model of psychological disturbance that I use in my work, 'C' stands for 'consequences'. These are emotional (unhealthy negative emotions), behavioural (unconstructive) and cognitive (highly distorted and ruminative thinking).

A.3 The ABC model of psychological health

I will present in this section, the model of psychological health I use in my work. Again this is expressed in an ABC framework (see the right-hand column in Table A.1).

'A'

As 'A' is the same in the ABC models of psychological health and disturbance, see my comments above on 'A'.

'B'

I use the term 'basic attitudes' at 'B' in the ABC framework, as noted above, with respect to both psychological disturbance and health. When they underpin a psychologically healthy response to adversity, these basic attitudes are considered to be flexible and non-extreme. Of the two, flexible attitudes are considered to be at the core of psychological health and non-extreme attitudes are considered to be derived from these flexible attitudes.

'C'

'C' stands for consequences in the ABC model of psychological health I use in my work. These consequences are emotional (healthy negative emotions), behavioural (constructive) and cognitive (realistic, balanced and non-ruminative thinking).

Notes

Chapter 1

1 As shown in Ellis and Joffe Ellis (2011), Ellis used a variety of terms to denote primary irrational beliefs including 'absolutistic thinking', 'rigid thinking', 'demandingness' and 'musturbation'. My own approach is different: I routinely use the term 'rigid attitudes' to denote attitudes at the core of psychological disturbance (see Appendix).
2 Sometimes Ellis stresses the 'nondemanding' aspects of primary rational beliefs; sometimes he doesn't. In the latter case he refers to them as 'preferences' and 'wants' (Ellis & Joffe Ellis, 2011). I routinely use the term 'flexible attitudes' to denote attitudes at the core of psychological health (see Appendix). I show throughout this book that the essence of these flexible attitudes is that they encourage possession and expression of one's preferences, but negate the idea that one must get one's preferences met. I see unmet preferences as adversities.

Chapter 2

1 Bordin's (1979) original formulation of the working alliance comprised three components: bonds, goals and tasks. I added the fourth component, 'views', later (Dryden, 2006, 2011b).
2 Currently often referred to as 'respect'.
3 A close reading of the Rogers (1957) paper shows that he only referred to the importance of the client's experience of the therapist's empathy and unconditional positive regard. He did not refer to the client's experience of the therapist's genuineness.
4 I concur with my REBT colleagues in generally preferring the term 'acceptance' to 'unconditional positive regard' or 'respect'. However, I am as much guided by my clients' preferences on this issue as I am my own when discussing such concepts with them, if relevant.
5 Privileging clients' viewpoints in such discussions is what Cooper and McLeod (2011) regard as a major principle of pluralism in counselling and psychotherapy.
6 One of the reasons that I did not renew my accreditation with the British Association for Behavioural and Cognitive Psychotherapy (BABCP) is because they would not count my attendance at non-CBT training events as continuing

professional development (CPD). This lack of flexibility was one of the reasons that led me to write this book, proving that good can come out of bad!

Chapter 3

1 Personally, I don't like the word 'case' in this context as it objectifies the client. However, it is in general use in the field and thus I will employ it in this book, albeit reluctantly.

Chapter 6

1 Known as 'Clue' in North America.
2 One of the major recent developments within the CBT tradition has been the growth of those CBT approaches that recommend that clients mindfully accept the presence of dysfunctional cognitions and troublesome feelings without engaging with them. This may be thought of as an acceptance-based focus (ABF) and is typical of what has become known as 'third-wave CBT'. I generally recommend that clients identify, question and change rigid, extreme attitudes (at 'B') in the ABC framework, and respond to distorted inferences (either at 'A' or at 'C'). In short, I recommend that clients mindfully engage with troublesome cognitions (i.e. inferences and attitudes) with the purpose of changing them. This may be known as a change-based focus (CBF). However, as we shall see, I also incorporate ABF strategies into my work as well.
3 In this section, I will mark and number the contexts as 'A1' etc., and Tina's responses and lack of responses as 'C1'etc.

Chapter 7

1 If you recall, I defined the personal domain – a term introduced by Beck (1976) – as 'a kind of psychological space that contains anything that the person deems to be personally valuable' (Dryden, 2011b: 25).
2 In this chapter and the next, I will use the case of Susan when I want to illustrate the points being made.
3 From an REBT perspective, DiGiuseppe (1991) argued that irrational and rational beliefs can be questioned with respect to their consistency with reality (empirical questioning), their logical sense (logical questioning) and their outcome for the person (pragmatic questioning). DiGiuseppe's analysis informs my thinking.
4 A 'cod liver oil' moment occurs in therapy when the therapist asks the client to accept something unpalatable that is beneficial for them in the longer term.
5 The reverse is also true that if the person can tolerate the uncertainty, doing so helps them to hold both positions regarding the diagnosis.

Appendix

1 This phrase was suggested by my friend and colleague, Walter Matweychuk.

References

Adler, A. (1927). *Understanding Human Nature*. New York: Garden City.

Bannister, D., & Fransella, F. (1986). *Inquiring Man: The Psychology of Personal Constructs*. London: Croom-Helm.

Barker, C., Pistrang, N., Shapiro, D.A., & Shaw, I. (1990). Coping and help-seeking in the UK adult population. *British Journal of Clinical Psychology*, 29, 271–85.

Beck, A.T. (1976). *Cognitive Therapy and the Emotional Disorders*. New York: International Universities Press.

Beutler, L.E., Malik, M., Alimohammed, S., Harwood, T.M., Talebi, H., Noble, S., & Wong, E. (2004). Therapist variables. In M.J. Lambert (ed.), *Bergin and Garfield's Handbook of Psychotherapy and Behavior Change*. 5th edition (pp. 227–306). New York: Wiley.

Blenkiron, P. (2010). *Stories and Analogies in Cognitive Behaviour Therapy*. Chichester: John Wiley & Sons.

Bond, F.W., & Dryden, W. (1996a). Why two central REBT hypotheses appear untestable. *Journal of Rational-Emotive and Cognitive Behaviour Therapy*, 14(1), 29–40.

Bond, F.W., & Dryden, W. (1996b). Testing an REBT theory: The effects of rational beliefs, irrational beliefs, and their control or certainty contents on the functionality of inferences, II: In a personal context. *International Journal of Psychotherapy*, 1(1), 55–77.

Bordin, E.S. (1979). The generalizability of the psychoanalytic concept of the working alliance. *Psychotherapy: Theory, Research and Practice*, 16, 252–60.

Burns, D.D. (1980). *Feeling Good: The New Mood Therapy*. New York: Morrow.

Colman, A. (2015). *Oxford Dictionary of Psychology*. 4th edition. Oxford: Oxford University Press.

Cooper, M., & McLeod, J. (2011). *Pluralistic Counselling and Psychotherapy*. London: Sage.

Cuijpers, P., Geraedts, A.S., van Oppen, P., Andersson, G., Markowitz, J.C., & van Straten, A. (2011). Interpersonal psychotherapy for depression: A meta-analysis. *American Journal of Psychiatry*, 168(6), 581–92.

References

DiGiuseppe, R. (1991). Comprehensive cognitive disputing in rational-emotive therapy. In M. Bernard (ed.), *Using Rational-Emotive Therapy Effectively* (pp. 173–95). New York: Plenum.

Dorn, F.J. (ed.). (1984). *The Social Influence Process in Counseling and Psychotherapy*. Springfield, IL: Charles C. Thomas.

Dryden, W. (1985). Challenging but not overwhelming: A compromise in negotiating homework assignments. *British Journal of Cognitive Psychotherapy*, 3(1), 77–80.

Dryden, W. (1990). Self-disclosure in rational-emotive therapy. In G. Stricker & M.N. Fisher (eds), *Self-Disclosure in the Therapeutic Relationship* (pp. 61–74). New York: Plenum.

Dryden, W. (1997). *Therapists' Dilemmas*. Revised edition. London: Sage.

Dryden, W. (1999a). *How to Accept Yourself*. London: Sheldon.

Dryden, W. (1999b). Beyond LFT and discomfort disturbance: The case for the term 'non-ego disturbance'. *Journal of Rational-Emotive and Cognitive-Behavior Therapy*, 17(3), 165–200.

Dryden, W. (2000). *Overcoming Anxiety*. London: Sheldon.

Dryden, W. (2004). *Rational Emotive Behaviour Therapy: Clients' Manual*. London: Whurr.

Dryden, W. (2006). *Counselling in a Nutshell*. London: Sage.

Dryden, W. (2011a). *Manage Your Anxiety through CBT*. London: Hodder Education.

Dryden, W. (2011b). *Counselling in a Nutshell*. 2nd edition. London: Sage.

Dryden, W. (2016). *Attitudes in Rational Emotive Behaviour Therapy: Components, Characteristics and Adversity-Related Consequences*. London: Rationality Publications.

Dryden, W. (2018). *Cognitive-Emotive-Behavioural Coaching: A Flexible and Pluralistic Approach*. Abingdon, Oxon: Routledge.

Dryden, W., DiGiuseppe, R., & Neenan, M. (2010). *A Primer on Rational Emotive Behavior Therapy*. 3rd edition. Champaign, IL: Research Press.

Dryden, W., & Neenan, M. (2011). *Working with Resistance in Rational Emotive Behaviour Therapy*. Hove: Routledge.

Eck, D. (2006). *What Is Pluralism*. http://pluralism.org/what-is-pluralism/.

Egan, G. (2014). *The Skilled Helper: A Client Centred Approach*. EMEA edition. Andover, Hampshire: Cengage Learning EMEA.

Ellis, A. (1977). Fun as psychotherapy. *Rational Living*, 12(1), 2–6.

Ellis, A. (2002). *Overcoming Resistance: A Rational Emotive Behavior Therapy Integrated Approach*. New York: Springer.

Ellis, A., & Dryden, W. (1997). *The Practice of Rational Emotive Behavior Therapy*. 2nd edition. New York: Springer.

Ellis, A, & Joffe Ellis, D. (2011). *Rational Emotive Behavior Therapy*. Washington, DC: American Psychological Association.

Emmelkamp, P.M.G. (2013). Behavior therapy with adults. In M.J. Lambert (ed.), *Bergin and Garfield's Handbook of Psychotherapy and Behavior Change* (pp. 343–92). Hoboken, NJ: John Wiley & Sons.

References 139

Frankl, V. (1984). *Man's Search for Meaning: An Introduction to Logotherapy.* New York: Simon & Schuster.

Freud, A. (1946). *The Ego and the Mechanisms of Defense.* American edition. New York: International Universities Press.

Hollon, S.D., & Beck, A.T. (2013). Cognitive and cognitive-behavioral therapies. In M.J. Lambert (ed.), *Bergin and Garfield's Handbook of Psychotherapy and Behavior Change* (pp. 393–442). Hoboken, NJ: John Wiley & Sons.

Hutchins, D.E. (1984). Improving the counseling relationship. *Personnel and Guidance Journal,* 62, 572–5.

Iveson, C., George, E., & Ratner, H. (2012). *Brief Coaching: A Solution-Focused Approach.* Hove, East Sussex: Routledge.

Jacobs, M. (2017). *Psychodynamic Counselling in Action.* 5th edition. London: Sage.

Kellogg, S. (2015). *Transformational Chairwork: Using Psychotherapeutic Dialogues in Clinical Practice.* Lanham, MD: Rowman & Littlefield.

Kiesler, D.J. (1996). *Contemporary Interpersonal Theory and Research: Personality, Psychopathology, and Psychotherapy.* New York: John Wiley & Sons.

Law, D., & Jacob, J. (2015). *Goals and Goal Based Outcomes (GBOs): Some Useful Information.* 3rd edition. London: CAMHS Press.

Lazarus, A.A. (1989). *The Practice of Multi-Modal Therapy: Systematic, Comprehensive and Effective Psychotherapy.* Baltimore, MD: The Johns Hopkins University Press.

Leahy, R.L. (2007). Schematic mismatch in the therapeutic relationship. In P. Gilbert & R.L. Leahy (eds), *The Therapeutic Relationship in the Cognitive Behavioral Psychotherapies* (pp. 229–54). Hove, East Sussex: Routledge.

Leahy, R.L. (2017). *Cognitive Therapy Techniques: A Practitioner's Guide.* 2nd edition. New York: Guilford Press.

Lemma, A. (1999). *Humour on the Couch: Exploring Humour in Psychotherapy and in Everyday Life.* London: Whurr.

Lipton, P. (2004). *Inference to the Best Explanation.* 2nd edition. Abingdon, Oxon: Routledge.

Mackrill, T. (2011). Differentiating life goals and therapeutic goals: Expanding our understanding of the working alliance. *British Journal of Guidance & Counselling,* 39, 25–39.

Maultsby, M.C. (1975). *Help Yourself to Happiness through Rational Self-Counseling.* New York: Institute for Rational-Emotive Therapy.

Miranda, R., & Andersen, S. (2007). The therapeutic relationship: Implications from the social-cognitive process of transference. In P. Gilbert & R.L. Leahy (eds), *The Therapeutic Relationship in the Cognitive Behavioral Psychotherapies* (pp. 63–89). Hove, East Sussex: Routledge.

Narcotics Anonymous (1976). *NA White Booklet.* Chatsworth, CA: Narcotics Anonymous World Services, Inc.

Rachman, S.J., & Wilson, G.T. (1980). *The Effects of Psychological Therapy.* 2nd enlarged edition. New York: Pergamon.

140 References

Rogers, C.R. (1957). The necessary and sufficient conditions of therapeutic personality change. *Journal of Consulting Psychology*, 21, 95–103.

Safran, J.D., & Muran, J.C. (2000). *Negotiating the Therapeutic Alliance: A Relational Treatment Guide*. New York: Guilford.

Seabury, B., Seabury, B., & Garvin, C.D. (2011). *Foundations of Interpersonal Practice in Social Work: Promoting Competence in Generalist Practice*. Thousand Oaks, CA: Sage.

Stiles, W.B., Shapiro, D.A., & Elliott, R. (1986). Are all psychotherapies equivalent? *American Psychologist*, 41(2), 165–80.

Wampold, B.E., & Imel, Z.E. (2015). *The Great Psychotherapy Debate: The Evidence for What Makes Psychotherapy Work*. 2nd edition. New York: Routledge.

Index

ABC framework 27, 78, 127, 132–4; change-based focus 125, 136n2; client's openness to 60; exploration stage 112; goals 36–7, 38, 40; therapist's tasks 59
absolutistic thinking 2
acceptance 4, 17, 56–7, 90, 96, 103–9, 124, 132, 135n4
acceptance-based focus (ABF) 74, 125–6, 136n2
action, taking 85, 96–7, 123–4
active interpersonal style 11, 12, 13
adaptability 89
Adler, Alfred 32
adversity ('A') 132–3; accuracy of inferences 38; balanced realistic approach 86; behavioural responses 75–6; change-based focus 125; discomfort intolerance vs discomfort tolerance attitudes 97–8, 100, 103; distorted inferences 73–4; goals 33–5, 37–40, 41–2, 43–4, 112; healthy responses to 40; negative evaluation of 91–2; preferences 79–80; taking action in the face of 85, 96–7; target problems 36–7
affect 53
Andersen, S. 16
anger 42, 53–4
anxiety 36–8, 42, 43; ability to execute tasks 52; perpetuation of 51; public speaking 57–8, 62–71, 80, 84, 92–102, 105–8, 123; stammering 56

applicant role 20, 110
assertiveness 54
attitudes: choice of 78–85; 'interpersonal stance' 77; therapist styles when working with 54–7; vs beliefs 131–2; *see also* basic attitudes; extreme attitudes; flexible attitudes; non-extreme attitudes; rigid attitudes
authenticity 14
avoidance 51
awfulising attitudes 3, 90, 91–6, 132

balanced cognitions 8
balanced realistic approach 86
Barker, C. 28
basic attitudes ('B') 132–4; change-based focus 125; goals 40; target problems 36–7; use of the term 132
BASIC ID 53
Beck, Aaron T. 11, 55, 136n1
behaviour: adaptability 89; behavioural modality 53–4; change 122–4; context created by 75–7
beliefs 131–2, 135n1, 136n3
'best bet' 43, 65
Beutler, L.E. 112
'Big I-Little i' technique 118–19
'black and white' thinking 2
bonds vii, 9–17; cognitive-experiential understanding 121; 'core conditions' 9–10; counter-transference 16–17; engagement stage 111; influence 15–16; interpersonal style 10–14; transference 16

142 Index

Bordin, Ed vi, 9, 18, 135n1
'both/and' thinking 8, 88
British Association of Behavioural and Cognitive Psychotherapy (BABCP) 135n6
Burns, D.D. 8

cancellation policy 23
capabilities 48–9, 115
case conceptualisation 29, 121–2
CBT *see* Cognitive Behaviour Therapy
change 110–30; behavioural 122–4; cognitive-experiential understanding 114–26; devaluation vs unconditional acceptance attitudes 109; ending therapy 128; engagement 110–11; exploration 111–14; negative evaluations 92, 105; obstacles to 59, 60, 128–30; philosophical 124–5; preferences 80; tasks during stages of change 58–60; 'working for change' principle 46; working through 126–7
change-based focus (CBF) 74, 125–6, 136n2
choice 78–85; awfulising vs non-awfulising attitudes 91–6; devaluation vs unconditional acceptance attitudes 103–9; discomfort intolerance vs discomfort tolerance attitudes 97–103
client involvement vii, 10, 47
client role 20
client-therapist 'fit' 10–11
coaching 45
cognition 53–4, 89, 122
Cognitive Behaviour Therapy (CBT) vii, 5, 21, 112, 125, 136n2; *see also* Flexibility-Based Cognitive Behaviour Therapy
cognitive distortions 8, 73–4, 125–6
cognitive-experiential understanding 114–26
Cognitive Therapy (CT) 11, 55
collaborative approach 11
Colman, A. 132

'colouring process' 65, 70–3
comfort-oriented action 123
commitment-based action 124
communication 18, 114
concern 42, 95–6
confidence 50
confidentiality 19, 24, 26, 111
consent, negotiated 18–20, 23
consequences ('C') 132–4; change-based focus 125–6; client's behaviour 75–6; distorted inferences 73–4; goals 33, 39, 40; target problems 36–7
context 61–77; cognitive distortions 73–4; 'colouring process' 70–3; created by client's own behaviour 75–7; descriptions about 63, 64; inferences about 63, 64–75; specific or general 61–3
Cooper, M. 8, 135n5
coping model of self-disclosure 56
coping strategies 51
'core conditions' 9–10
'counselling as influence' 15
counselling skills 113–14
counter-transference 16–17
credibility 15, 16

dangerous goals 35–6
depression 42, 51, 52
devaluation attitudes 3, 56–7, 90, 103–9, 132
dialectical enquiry 82–5, 94, 100–1, 107
diaries 127
didactic approach 55
DiGiuseppe, R. 54, 55, 136n3
disagreement 18, 62, 69
disappointment 42
discomfort intolerance attitudes 3, 90, 97–103, 132
discomfort tolerance attitudes 4, 90, 96, 97–103, 132
dissatisfaction 41, 42–4
distorted inferences 73–4
disturbance: 'addressing disturbance' goals 33–4, 41–2; emotional 55, 67, 84, 95; psychological 2, 80, 92, 98–9, 105, 132–3

Index 143

diversity 88
doubts, reservations and objections (DROs) 84–5, 96, 102–3, 109, 129
Dr Phil 84

eclecticism 5, 6
Egan, G. 112
'either/or' thinking 8, 88
Ellis, Albert 2, 6, 8, 16, 135n1, 135n2
emotional disturbance 55, 67, 84, 95
emotional pain 103
emotions: cognitive-experiential understanding 116; modalities 53; negative 34, 39, 40, 41–2, 132, 133
empathy 10, 112, 128
enactive approach 56–7
ending therapy 59, 128
engagement 110–11
enquirer role 19–20
environment 113
envy 42
Epictetus 7, 78
evidence 64–5, 69–70
exceptions 87
excuses 129–30
expertise vii, 15–16, 52, 114
explicit communication 18
exploration 111–14
extra-therapy contact 23
extreme attitudes 2–3, 22, 30, 78, 90–109; ABC framework 132, 133; awfulising attitudes 3, 90, 91–6, 132; change-based focus 125–6; cognitive-experiential understanding 114; devaluation attitudes 3, 56–7, 90, 103–9, 132; discomfort intolerance attitudes 3, 90, 97–103, 132; doubts, reservations and objections 129; examination of 49, 50; public speaking 58; self-disclosure 56; Socratic questioning 55; see also rigid attitudes

fallibility 4, 8, 57, 105–8
familiarity, need for 77
FCBT see Flexibility-Based Cognitive Behaviour Therapy
feedback 10, 25, 32, 120

fees 23, 24
flexibility: choice of attitude 79, 80–1; concept of 1, 2; 'counselling as influence' 15; impact on psychological functioning 3–4; mindset 85–9; practice of FCBT 6–7; preferences 34, 80–1; psychotherapeutic approaches 5; therapeutic practice 6; see also flexible attitudes
Flexibility-Based Cognitive Behaviour Therapy (FCBT) vii, 1, 6–7; dialectical enquiry 82, 100; pluralism 7–8; reflection process 10; tasks 58, 59
flexible attitudes 22, 30, 78, 135n2; ABC framework 132, 133–4; brief version for clients 120; choice of 79–85; cognitive-experiential understanding 114; doubts, reservations and objections 84–5, 129; formulation of 49; inferences 66–9, 70, 73; modalities 54; self-disclosure 56; Socratic questioning 55; taking action 85; see also flexibility; non-extreme attitudes
formality 11, 12
frame of mind 52
Frankl, Victor 78–9
Freud, Anna 121
Freud, Sigmund 77

Garvin, C.D. 19
generalisation 63, 126–7
genuineness 10
goals vii, 9, 25, 27, 32–45; 'addressing dissatisfaction' 41, 42–4; 'addressing disturbance' 33–4, 41–2; client's perspective on 32–6; cognitive-experiential understanding 122; engagement stage 111; exploration stage 112; goal-directed action 123; pragmatic standpoint 84, 95, 102, 108; 'promoting development' 44–5; tasks and 48, 57, 58; therapist's perspective on 36–40
'grey' thinking 2
guilt 42

144 Index

habitual action 123
health, psychological 2, 80, 92, 98–9, 105, 132, 133–4
healthy attitude-based action 123
healthy body-based action 123
healthy negative emotions 34, 39, 40, 41, 132, 134
homework 50, 58, 59, 115–16
honesty 25, 26
humility 17
humour 11, 12, 14, 55–6, 119
hurt 42, 75–6
Hutchins, D.E. 52–3

imagery 53–4, 85, 97, 116, 120, 127
indifference 35, 67–8
inferences: accuracy of 38, 43, 65; change-based focus 125; 'colouring process' 65, 70–3; context 64–75; distorted 73–4; functional behavioural responses 76; inferential thinking 3, 4; 'interpersonal stance' 77
influence, bonds of 15–16
interest 113
interpersonal relationships 53–4
'interpersonal stance' 76–7
interpersonal style 10–14, 54–7

Jacob, J. 35–6
jealousy 42
Joffe Ellis, D. 135n1

Kelly, George 10, 12, 57

language, use of 52–3, 116–17
lapses 127
Law, D. 35–6
Lazarus, Arnold 13, 14, 53
Leahy, R.L. 16
learning styles 57–8, 117
length of therapy sessions 22
life, acceptance vs devaluation of 104–9, 132
life goals 44–5
Life History Questionnaire (LHQ) 13
listening 113, 116

logical sense standpoint 83, 136n3; awfulising vs non-awfulising attitudes 94, 95; devaluation vs unconditional acceptance attitudes 107, 108; discomfort intolerance vs discomfort tolerance attitudes 101–2
long-term perspective 87

Mackrill, T. 44
mastery model of self-disclosure 56
Maultsby, Maxie C. 64
McLeod, J. 8, 135n5
metaphorical approach 55, 120
mindsets 54–7, 78, 85–9
Miranda, R. 16
modalities 53–4, 57–8
modes 52–3

National Institute of Health and Care Excellence (NICE) 51
negative evaluations 91–3, 94, 95, 104–5, 106–7
negotiated consent 18–20, 23
Niebuhr, Reinhold 42
non-awfulising attitudes 4, 90, 91–6, 102, 132
non-extreme attitudes 4, 22, 30, 78, 90–109; ABC framework 132, 133–4; brief version for clients 120; cognitive-experiential understanding 114; discomfort tolerance attitudes 4, 90, 96, 97–103, 132; doubts, reservations and objections 129; formulation of 49; modalities 54; non-awfulising attitudes 4, 90, 91–6, 102, 132; Socratic questioning 55; unconditional acceptance attitudes 4, 56–7, 90, 96, 103–9, 124, 132; see also flexible attitudes
nondemanding thinking 2

obsessive-compulsive problems 51
obstacles to change 59, 60, 128–30
openness 25
optimism 86
others, acceptance vs devaluation of 104–9, 132

Index 145

pain, emotional 103
passivity 11, 13, 54
person-centred therapy 5
perspective 78, 86–7
pessimism 86
philosophical change 124–5
phobias 50
physiological functioning 53
pleasing others 123
pluralism vii, 5, 7–8, 135n5;
encouraging client pluralism 88;
tasks 47, 53
polarised thinking 70, 71
pragmatic standpoint 84, 136n3;
awfulising vs non-awfulising
attitudes 94, 95–6; devaluation vs
unconditional acceptance attitudes
107, 108–9; discomfort intolerance
vs discomfort tolerance attitudes
101, 102
preferences 79–82, 83
problem conceptualisation 19, 27–30
Procrustes 1–2
'promoting development' goals 44–5
psychoanalysis 7, 16
psychotherapeutic approaches 4–5
public speaking 35, 56, 57–8, 62–71,
80, 84, 92–102, 105–8, 123

questioning 114; Socratic 48, 55

Rational Emotive Behaviour Therapy
(REBT) vi, 2, 90, 124; attitudes vs
beliefs 131–2; inferences 66, 69;
interpersonal style 11; Socratic
questioning 55; treatment
sequence 5
reactant clients 14
reality standpoint 82–3, 136n3;
awfulising vs non-awfulising
attitudes 94–5; devaluation vs
unconditional acceptance attitudes
107, 108; discomfort intolerance vs
discomfort tolerance attitudes 101
REBT *see* Rational Emotive
Behaviour Therapy
recordings of sessions 24
reflection process 10, 25, 26, 27, 47
reflexivity 8

rehearsal 97
relapse prevention 59, 60, 127
remorse 42
repetition compulsion 77
resilience 101
responsibility 26, 60
rigid attitudes 22, 30, 78, 135n1;
ABC framework 132, 133;
change-based focus 125–6; choice
of 79–85; cognitive-experiential
understanding 114; distorted
cognitive consequences 74;
doubts, reservations and objections
84–5, 129; examination of 49, 50;
inferences 66–9, 70–3, 75; public
speaking 58; self-disclosure 56;
Socratic questioning 55; *see also*
extreme attitudes
rigidity 1–2; choice of attitude 79,
80–1; 'counselling as influence'
15; impact on psychological
functioning 2–3; inferences
coloured by 65, 70–3; practice of
FCBT 6–7; preferences 34, 80–1;
psychotherapeutic approaches 5;
therapeutic practice 5–6
Rogers, Carl 9–10, 135n3
role models 117

sadness 42
safety-seeking manoeuvres 85, 97
schemas 16–17
Seabury, B. 19
self-acceptance 4, 17, 56–7, 90, 96,
103–9, 124, 132
self-actualisation 8
self-compassion 17
self-deception 129–30
self-devaluation 3, 56–7, 90,
103–9, 132
self-disclosure 11–12, 56, 119–20
self-help 117, 127
self-worth 70
sensation 53–4
Serenity Prayer 42, 124
session length 22
shame 17, 42
short-term perspective 87
skills 48, 49, 115, 123

146 Index

SMART goals 33
Socratic questioning 48, 55
solutions approach 87
sorrow 42
stammering 56
strengths 58, 117
struggle 97–100, 101–2
summarising 114

target problems 27, 30–1; choice of
attitude 79; client's perspective on
goals 32–6; specific context 62–3;
therapist's perspective on goals
36–7
tasks vii, 9, 25–6, 27, 46–60;
client's learning style and
preferred modalities 57–8;
cognitive-experiential
understanding 121; engagement
stage 111; getting the most out of
58; homework 50, 58, 59, 115–16;
selection of 47; stages of change
58–60; therapist styles 54–7;
varying the use of 52–4; working
alliance perspective 46–52
therapeutic potency 50
therapist authenticity 14
therapist styles 10–14, 54–7
Thinking-Feeling-Action
(TFA) 52–3
transference 16
treatment plans 54
treatment sequence 5
trust 15, 16, 121

uncertainty 72, 88, 136n5
unconditional acceptance attitudes 4,
56–7, 90, 96, 103–9, 124, 132
unconditional positive regard 10

unhealthy negative emotions 34,
39–40, 41–2, 132, 133
unrealistic goals 35–6

values 119, 124
views vii, 9, 18–31; addressing
problems 30–1; client's choice of
therapeutic approach 20–1; client's
contributions to therapy 25–6;
cognitive-experiential understanding
121–2; confidentiality 24;
engagement stage 111; explaining
the way of working 22; explicit
communication 18; exploration
stage 112; negotiated consent
18–20; practicalities of therapy
22–3; problem conceptualisation
27–30; therapist's contributions to
therapy 26–7
visual diagrams 117–19
vulnerability factors 59, 60, 127

warmth 14
weaknesses 58
well-being 26
working alliance vi–vii, 9, 24–5, 59;
addressing problems 31; client
learning 57; client-therapist 'fit'
10–11; client's perspective on
goals 32; cognitive-experiential
understanding 121–2; context
62, 63; engagement stage 111;
examination of inferences 69;
goals 41; humour 55; problem
conceptualisation 30; tasks
46–52; transference and
counter-transference 16
'working for change' 46
working through 126–7